ST. COSMAS AITOLOS

Ἀπολυτίκιον. Ἦχος γ'.

Θ είας πίστεως διδασκαλίᾳ, κατεκόσμησας τὴν Ἐκκλησίαν, ζηλωτὴς τῶν Ἀποστόλων γενόμενος· σὺ γὰρ τῇ θείᾳ ἀγάπῃ πτερούμενος, Εὐαγγελίου τὸν λόγον διέσπειρας. Κοσμᾶ ἔνδοξε, Χριστὸν τὸν Θεὸν ἱκέτευε, δωρήσασθαι ἡμῖν τὸ μέγα ἔλεος.

Κοντάκιον. Ἦχος γ'. Ἡ Παρθένος σήμερον.

Π ολιτείαν ἄμεμπτον, διαδραμὼν ἐν τῷ Ἄθῳ, ὡς Μωσῆς ἠξίωσαι, τῆς θεϊκῆς ἐμφανείας· ἔνθεν δή, τὴν Ἐκκλησίαν καταφαιδρύνεις, πράξεσι, καὶ θεηγόροις σου Πάτερ λόγοις, ὑπὲρ ἧς καὶ ἐναθλήσας, διπλοῖς στεφάνοις, Κοσμᾶ κεκόσμησαι.

Μεγαλυνάριον

Χ αίροις Ἀποστόλων ὁ μιμητής, καὶ τῆς Ἐκκλησίας, ὁ διδάσκαλος καὶ φωστήρ· χαίροις εὐσεβείας, ὁ θεῖος φυτοκόμος, καὶ κοινωνὸς Μαρτύρων Κοσμᾶ ἰσάγγελε.

Apolytikion.

By teaching the Divine Faith, thou hast richly adorned the Church and become a zealous emulator of the Apostles; for having been lifted up by the wings of divine love, thou hast spread far and wide the message of the Gospel. O glorious Cosmas, entreat God that He grant us His great mercy.

Kontakion.

Having led an irreproachable life on Athos, like Moses thou hast been deemed worthy of God's manifestation; wherefore truly thou dost gladden the Church exceedingly by thy deeds and thy God-inspired words, O Father Cosmas, having contended for which, thou hast been adorned with a double crown.

Megalynarion.

Rejoice thou emulator of the Apostles, teacher and luminary of the Church; rejoice thou divine cultivator of piety, associate of Martyrs and peer of Angels.

MODERN ORTHODOX SAINTS

1

ST. COSMAS AITOLOS

Great Missionary, Awakener, Illuminator, and holy Martyr of Greece. An account of his Life, Character and Message, including his teaching on God, Heaven and Hell, and his Prophecies, together with Selections from his Sermons.

By

CONSTANTINE CAVARNOS

Third Edition
Revised and considerably enlarged

INSTITUTE FOR BYZANTINE
AND MODERN GREEK STUDIES
115 Gilbert Road
Belmont, Massachusetts 02178
U.S.A.

First edition 1971
Second edition 1975
Third, revised and considerably enlarged, edition 1985
All rights reserved
Copyright, © 1971, 1985, by Constantine Cavarnos
Published by THE INSTITUTE FOR BYZANTINE
AND MODERN GREEK STUDIES, INC.
115 Gilbert Road, Belmont, Massachusetts 02178, U.S.A.
Library of Congress Catalog Card Number: 85-80440

Complete set ISBN 0-914744-12-7
This volume clothbound ISBN 0-914744-64-X
This volume paperbound ISBN 0-914744-65-8
Fourth printing, February 1994

Fifth printing, October 2002

PREFACE

The present work is the first of a projected series on modern Eastern Orthodox Saints. Among other volumes that will follow will be one on Macarios of Corinth (1731-1805), one on Nicodemos the Hagiorite (1749-1809), one on Saraphim of Sarov (1759-1833), and one on Nectarios of Aegina (1846-1920), all of them very outstanding figures of recent Orthodox spirituality.

I was prompted to inaugurate this series by the awareness of the paucity of English-language publications dealing with Orthodox saints and the realization of the great value such works have for awakening us spiritually and guiding us in the path of true religion. Saints are the spiritual aristocracy of the Church, and it is to them that men must turn in order to find their bearings, especially in a period of great confusion and overwhelming materialism and unbelief such as the present age.

The Introductory, in which I point out the main features of St. Cosmas' life, character and teaching, has appeared in *St. Vladimir's Seminary Quarterly,* Vol. X, No. 4 (1966). It is reprinted here with some revisions and additions. The rest of the volume, comprising my annotated translation of the Life of the Saint by his disciple Sapphiros Christodoulidis and of the passages which I have selected from his *Teachings,* appear in print for the first time.

CONSTANTINE CAVARNOS

March, 1971

PREFACE TO THE THIRD EDITION

When the second edition (1975) of this volume was out of print, I undertook to prepare the text for a third, considerably augmented, edition. The second edition was simply a reprint of the first, except for a number of corrections of typographical errors, whereas the present one contains the following new texts: (1) The Apolytikon, Kontakion, and Megalynarion of St. Cosmas, taken from the service composed in honor of him by the eminent hymnographer Gerasimos Micragiannanitis, of the Skete of St. Anne on Mount Athos. (2) A page of sayings regarding the "Value of Reading Lives of Saints," which I culled from various writers. (3) Two essays that I have written on St. Cosmas' teaching, one "On God" and the other "On Heaven and Hell." (4) A chapter containing some of the "Prophecies of the Saint." And (5) a "Selected Bibliography." "On God" has been published in the *The Greek Orthodox*

Theological Review, Vol. XXV, No. 2 (1980). "On Heaven and Hell" appears in print for the first time. So does my translation of the passages on the value of reading lives of saints and the chapter on the prophecies, as well as the bibliography.

I owe thanks to Dr. John Johnstone, Jr., for having read the new texts in this edition in manuscript form and suggested a number of improvements.

CONSTANTINE CAVARNOS

CONTENTS

VALUE OF READING LIVES OF SAINTS

Cleave to the saints, for they who cleave to them shall be made holy.

— St. Clement of Rome

Just as painters in working from models constantly gaze at their exemplar and thus strive to transfer the expression of the original to their own artistry, so too he who is anxious to make himself perfect in all kinds of virtue must gaze upon the lives of the saints as upon statues, so to speak, that move and act, and must make their excellence his own by imitation.

— St. Basil the Great

Blessed is he who plants in his soul good plants, that is, the virtues and the lives of saints.

— St. Ephraim the Syrian

A person is touched more profoundly and benefits more by reading one beautiful life of a saint than by discourses and philosophies.

— Agapios Landos of Athos

For the Christian, there is no teaching that is more efficacious than reading the life of a saint, especially of one who has lived in his own time.

— Photios Kontoglou

INTRODUCTORY

St. Cosmas Aitolos is undoubtedly the greatest missionary of modern Greece, and may with good reason be called the Father of the modern Greek nation. He played a role of supreme importance in the moral and religious awakening and enlightenment of the Greeks during the second half of the eighteenth century, and thus more than anyone else inaugurated the modern Greek era. Cosmas was leading a life of spiritual endeavor at the Monastery of Philotheou on the Holy Mountain of Athos when he felt called by God to undertake the mission of regenerating his fellow Christians. The Greeks had fallen into great ignorance; and ignorance, this Saint believed, as did Socrates and Plato in Antiquity, meant ungodliness and perdition. Education, enlightenment was needed. After having lived on Mount Athos for seventeen years, he sought and obtained the consent of his Elders in 1760 to leave the monastery and go to Constantinople, there to obtain a permit from the Patriarch to preach. At Constantinople he met the Patriarch Seraphim II (1757-1761), who, upon learning of Cosmas' desire and seeing his zeal, appointed him a "Preacher of the Nation" and gave him a written permit to preach throughout the Greek world.

Eastern Orthodox monasticism has always flourished in the desert, in the quiet of the wilderness, and has looked upon seclusion as one of the necessary conditions for the spiritual progress of the monk. It has regarded the monk's entry into the world as fraught with serious dangers. Aitolos' decision to leave the monastery and return to the world in order to preach did not result from his feeling that this standpoint was wrong. In one of his sermons he stresses his belief that a monk must live far from the world, if he is to achieve salvation. He reconciled this stand with his own abandonment of monastic seclusion by saying that he was willing to sacrifice himself for the salvation of his brethren and that perhaps God's mercy would save him, also: "My brethren, I act wrongly in this regard, but as our race has fallen into ignorance, I said, Let Christ lose me, one sheep, and gain the others.' Perhaps God's mercy and your prayers will save me, too."[1] One recalls here St. Paul's statement: "I could wish that I myself were accursed from Christ for the sake of my brethren."[2] Only a man truly called to become an Apostle could be so disposed and make such a remark. It is to be noted that the Greeks have regarded St. Cosmas Aitolos as an *Isapostolos,* a "Peer of the Apostles."

His mission as an itinerant preacher began when he was forty-six years of age and continued until the time of his martyrdom at the hands of the Turks on August 24, 1779. For twenty years Cosmas traveled throughout the Greek mainland, the Dodecanese and Ionian Islands, and elsewhere, preaching and establishing schools. He addressed large audiences, mostly outdoors, explaining to them the basic doctrines of Eastern Orthodoxy, dissuading the people from wickedness, exhorting them to lead a godly life, stressing the need for instruction in the true Faith, and establishing schools in many villages and towns. From one of his letters, written shortly before his martyrdom, we learn that he established two hundred "common," elementary schools, and ten "Greek" or higher schools. Moreover, he gave away books by the Greek Church Fathers and catechisms, baptismal basins, prayer-ropes, and little crosses, which he persuaded the well-to-do to provide him with for free distribution to the Christians.

Cosmas' sermons were exceedingly effective. They brought an immediate and profound inner transformation in his listeners. Not only the Christians, but Mohammedans also regarded him as a Saint, because of his inspiring sermons, his impeccable character, and the miraculous events which occurred at many places that he visited. His sermons, together with his ability as a leader and organizer, enabled him to found the large number of schools that we have noted.

Apart from thirteen letters, the Saint left no writings. His sermons were always extemporaneous. What we have of his teaching was committed to writing by ardent Christians who followed him in his journeys. The recorded sermons have been given the name *Didachai*, "Teachings," a term that brings to mind the early Christian manual entitled *Didache of the Twelve Apostles*, and reveals the deep reverence with which Cosmas' sermons have been regarded. The *Didachai* of Cosmas were read in the churches, both during his lifetime and after his death, for the edification of the congregations. A good many of his sermons were probably recorded, but only a small number has come down to us. In 1953, a painstaking researcher, Archimandrite Sophronios Papakyriakou, brought together nine *Didachai* in his book *Teaching, Letters, and Martyrdom of Cosmas the*

Aitolian, Holy Martyr and Peer of the Apostles. This is the largest collection of St. Cosmas' *Didachai* thus far to appear in print.

The language he used to convey his message was the vernacular Greek. He chose this language so that all who listened, both the old and the young, the literate and the illiterate, could understand him without any difficulty. His manner of expression, reflecting his personality, was characterized by great simplicity, directness, warmth, charm, and serenity. Of Aitolos' sermons one may say what the Apostle Paul says of his own: "My speech and my preaching are not with the plausible words of human wisdom, but in demonstration of the Spirit and of power. . . ."[3]

His teaching is based explicity on the Holy Scriptures, particularly the New Testament, and on the writings of the Greek Fathers. Both from his biography and his sermons, it is manifest that he assigned the highest importance to the study of Scripture and the works of the Church Fathers, and that he studied both very assiduously. In his life we read how he sought to find the will of God regarding his planned choice of vocation by consulting the Divine Scriptures. We read also that he studied the Greek Fathers and distributed their works to those who could read or who or who promised to learn to

read. In the *Didachai* we find the following very
revealing passages as well as others similar to them:
"Studying the Holy and Sacred Gospels, I found
many and varied ideas, which are all pearls, diamonds, treasures, wealth, joy, delight, eternal life."[4]
"What I have said, my brethren, are not my own
statements, but those of the Holy Spirit, taken from
Holy Scripture."[5] "We leave aside, my brethren, the
prattling of the impious, the heretics, and the
atheists, and say only what the Holy Spirit has
illumined the holy Prophets, Apostles, and Fathers
of the Church to write."[6] "The Holy Spirit illumined
firstly the holy Prophets, and they wrote the Divine
Scripture; secondly, He illumined the holy Apostles;
and thirdly, He has illumined the holy Fathers, and
they have explained the books of our Church, in
order that we may know how to conduct ourselves."[7]

St. Cosmas proclaimed the superiority of Orthodoxy over all the other Faiths. "I have searched the
depths of wisdom," he says. "This I have truly come
to realize, that all the Faiths are sham, only the Faith
of the Orthodox Christians is sound and holy ....
Rejoice that you are Orthodox Christians and weep
and mourn for the unbelievers and the heretics, who
walk in the dark."[8]

Remarkably consistent and clearcut, Aitolos'

teaching is focused on the means whereby man may achieve salvation. His preoccupation with establishing schools sprang from this fundamental religious concern. Education as envisaged by him should have as its chief aim to convey sound religious knowledge and lead to pious living. "The school," he remarks, "opens churches, the school opens monasteries."[9] "It is at school that we learn what God is, what the angels are, what the demons, paradise, hell, virtue, vice, the soul and the body are."[10]

The closely related problem of a well qualified, educated priesthood comes up in his sermons. Aitolos stresses that the priest bears a heavy responsibility for the moral and spiritual state of the Christians that have been entrusted to him, and will be held accountable for them on the day of Judgment. He who wants to become a priest must be a person of great purity, and must be properly educated, so that he may be able to exlain the Gospels and the rest of the Scriptures to the faithful. He should be ordained after reaching the age of thirty. Consonant with his vocation, the priest must not occupy himself with secular matters, but must always have his mind turned to things spiritual.

St. Cosmas indicates the practices through which

man may fare well in this life and attain blessedness in the life to come. Of greatest importance are repentance, confession, fasting, prayer, humility, love of God and of one's neighbor. He especially emphasizes humility and love. "The Christian," he says, "needs two wings in order to soar upward and attain Paradise: humility and love."[11] Humility is angelic, whereas pride is diabolic. The one leads to Paradise; the other, to Hell. In speaking of love of God and man, he stresses that without this love salvation is impossible. In connection with love of our fellow man, the Saint particularly exhorts his listeners to practice almsgiving, as a concrete and most important manifestation of such love. He remarks: "I have a loaf of bread to eat, while you do not; love tells me: Do not eat it alone, but give some to your brethren. I have clothes, while you do not; love tells me: Give one to your brother."[12] Cosmas reproaches those who live by exploitation and injustice, asserting that they are doomed to perdition, unless they repent and change their ways.

From his statements on prayer, which he also emphasizes, it is evident that the Saint was familiar with the great Byzantine tradition of mysticism known as *hesychasm,* and that he practiced the Jesus Prayer: "Lord Jesus Christ, Son of God, have mercy upon me." He enjoins upon his listeners to practice this prayer at all times.

Very noteworthy are his frequent remarks concerning God and man. He speaks of God as all light, all joy, all goodness, all mercy, all love. The attribute of God that he stresses above all others is love. "God", says Aitolos, "has many and diverse names: He is called Light, and Life, and Resurrection, and the Way. However, His chief name is and is said to be Love."[13] Thus both in the ethical and in the theological teaching of Cosmas love is central.

Man, the individual, is asserted to be more precious than the whole world. Man's worth comes from his psyche, his soul, which is immaterial and immortal, and chiefly constitutes man. The body is but the garment of the psyche. It is the psyche that sees, hears, talks, acquires knowledge, and gives life to the body. When the psyche withdraws from the body, the body disintegrates. Cosmas' statements about the human soul are at times strikingly reminiscent of Plato's. However, he is not a Platonist, who denies that the body is a part of human nature and who believes that after death the souls of the righteous will live forever in a disembodied state. At the end of time, Cosmas teaches, "God will resurrect all of mankind, with the souls and bodies."[14]

The Saint stresses that it is proper for the psyche to rule and for the body to obey. One is truly a man *(anthropos)* when this relationship holds. When the order is inverted, and the psyche becomes a slave of the body, then one should no longer be called a man but a beast.

From his deep Christian love springs Cosmas' profound concern for the good of the whole of mankind. In one of his sermons he says: "If it were possible for me, my brethren, to ascend to the sky and cry with a loud voice and preach to the whole world and say that our Christ is the Son and Logos of God and true God, and the life of all, I would do so. But inasmuch as I cannot do that great thing, I do this small one, and walk from place to place and teach my brethren according to my power."[15]

Human history is not for him exclusively the product of man's actions; God takes part in it. Cosmas sees Divine Providence in such events as the appearance of Constantine the Great, which resulted in the rise of a great Christian kingdom, the Byzantine, and the fall of this kingdom to the Turks. "Three hundred years after the resurrection of Christ," he says, "God sent us Saint Constantine and established a Christian kingdom; and the Christians had this kingdom for 1150 years. Then God took it from the Christians and brought the Turks, and gave it to them for our good; and the Turks now have it for 320 years. And why did God bring the Turks and not some other race? For our good, because the other nations would have caused detriment to our Faith."[16] The "other races" were the Europeans, who since the launching of the Crusades and the sacking of Constantinople by the Franks were generally regarded by the Greeks as their worst enemies.

Aitolos saw the hand of Providence not only in Greece's past and present, but also in her future. He prophesied that Greece would be liberated in the third generation and would have a great future. His prophecies in this regard stirred up the hopes of the Greeks and were one of the major factors that caused them to intensify their efforts for achieving Greece's independence.

The deep and extensive influence of St. Cosmas Aitolos did not come to an end when he died. It has continued uninterrupted to the present day through publications and through oral tradition of his teaching, miracles, and prophecies that is preserved at many of the places where he preached. The significant religious revival that took place in Greece during the middle of the nineteenth century was effected by three itinerant preachers: Phlamiatos, Lambropoulos, and Papoulakos, who were

CHURCH OF SAINT COSMAS AITOLOS

At Mega Dendron, the birthplace of the Saint. Founded in 1955.

CHURCH OF SAINT COSMAS AITOLOS

At the village of Sitaria in Phlorina, northern Greece.

inspired by his example. Today, among the eminent Greeks who evince the strong influence of St.
Cosmas are Metropolitan Augustine Kantiotis and
Archimandrite Haralambos Vasilopoulos. Kantiotis
is Metropolitan of Phlorina, in northern Greece, the
editor of two vigorous religious periodicals, *Spitha,*
"Spark," and *Stavros,* "Cross," and author of *Saint
Cosmas Aitolos* and of many other edifying books,
while Vasilopoulos, formerly Abbot of the Monastery of Petraki at Athens, is the editor of the
remarkable semimonthly *Orthodoxos Typos,* "Orthodox Press," and of numerous books, including one
entitled *Cosmas Aitolos, the Greek Missionary.* In his
book on the Saint, Kantiotis remarks that "through
his saintly life, his inspiring teaching, his miracles
and prophecies, Cosmas benefited the Greeks more
than anyone else during the eighteenth century."[17]
Vasilopoulos gives this estimate of the Saint: "Aitolos
is one of the great Christian and national figures
of Greece. He is the Missionary of the Balkans. He
is something more: he is the Peer of the Apostles,
as he has been named by the Church."[18] Father
Vasilopoulos calls Cosmas "the Missionary of the
Balkans" because his influence has not been limited
to Greece, as he also preached in Constantinople
and in Albania and South Serbia, and reports of
him and his teaching spread elsewhere in the Balkan
nations.

A very impressive picture of Saint Cosmas' influence among the Greeks as evidenced in writings is given by Kostas Sardelis' *Analytic Bibliography of Cosmas Aitolos (1765-1967)*.[19] This work lists more than thirty books and six hundred articles dealing with Aitolos.

That his influence is growing is testified not only by the increased number of writings on him in recent years, but also by the fact that he was officially declared a Saint by the Oecumenical Patriarchate at Constantinople on April 20, 1961, that many churches have since then been erected and named after him, and that on May 17, 1970, a large icon depicting him was officially placed during the Divine Liturgy in the Metropolitan Church of Athens, on a special, beautifully carved icon-stand.

The sentiments of the Orthodox towards St. Cosmas are well expressed by the following Apolytikion, which was recently composed by the eminent Athonite hymnographer Gerasimos Micragiannanitis, and is now part of the akoluthia that is chanted in his honor on August 24:

> "By teaching the Divine Faith, thou hast richly adorned the Church and become a zealous emulator of the Apostles; for having been lifted up by the wings of divine

love, thou hast spread far and wide the message of the Gospel. O glorious Cosmas, entreat God that He grant us His great mercy."[20]

THE LIFE OF ST. COSMAS

By Sapphiros Christodoulidis, His Disciple[1]

This true man of God, Cosmas, Teacher and Preacher of the Divine Gospel, was a native of a small village of Aitolia named Mega Dendron. The son of pious parents, he was brought up and educated[2] "in the nurture and admonition of the Lord," as the Apostle says.[3]

When he was twenty years of age, perhaps older, he began to teach grammar under the deacon Ananias Dervisanos.[4]

As the school of Vatopedi[5] on the Holy Mountain began to function at that time and reports about it spread widely, he went there with many of his former fellow students. Here he studied language

and literature under the teacher Panagiotis Palamas.
Then he received instruction in logic by the teacher
Nicholas Tzartzoulios of Metsovo, who became the
head of the school after the great savant Eugene.[6]
He was still a layman, named Constas. Yet, although dressed as a layman, he was adorned with
the gravity of a monk, disciplined himself in everything, and strove after perfect ascesis.[7]

When the famous school was, unfortunately,
deserted, the teachers having left, good Constas
departed[8] and went to the holy Monastery of Philotheou.[9] Here he was tonsured a monk [10] and eagerly
submitted to the hardships of the monastic life.
Later, when the monastery was in need of a priest,
he yielded to the strong entreaties of the fathers and
was ordained a priest-monk. The blessed one had
an intense desire in his heart, from the time he was
a layman, to benefit his fellow Christians through
what he had learned. And often he said that our
Christian brothers are in great need of the word of
God, and that it is the duty of those who become
educated not to run to the houses and the courts
of the powerful, and nullify their education in order
to acquire wealth and high offices, but to teach
especially the common people, who live in great
ignorance and barbarism, and thus to gain a
heavenly reward and unwithering glory. However,

despite the intense desire and zeal that burned in his holy heart to benefit the many, reflecting how great and difficult an undertaking Apostolic preaching is, being humble and modest he did not venture to attempt it of himself, without becoming convinced that it was in accord with the will of God. Therefore, wishing to test and see if this was the will of God, he opened the Divine Scripture, and behold the miracle! There was found at once before him the saying of the Apostle: "Let no one seek his own, but each one another's also."[11] That is, let no one seek only his own good, but also the good of his brother. Having been thus informed and having revealed his aim to other spiritual fathers and received their consent, he went to Constantinople,[12] in order to meet his brother Chrysanthos, who was a teacher.[13] The latter instructed him a little in the art of rhetoric, so that he might know how to speak somewhat methodically. At the same time the Saint revealed his thoughts to the most pious bishops and teachers there, and finding them unanimously inciting him towards this divine work, he received from the Patriarch of Constantinople Seraphim a written permit to preach.

Thus the blessed monk began to preach the Gospel of the Kingdom of Heaven, first in the churches and villages of Constantinople. From there he went to Naupaktos, Vrachori, Mesolongi and other places, and then back to Constantinople. Here he consulted with the Patriarch of that time, Sophronios, and received from him a new permit and his blessing. Then he began preaching again the word of the Gospel with increased warmth and zeal. He visited nearly all of the Dodecanese islands and taught the Christians to repent and do works worthy of repentance. Thence he went to the Holy Mountain of Athos, about 1775, and having visited the monasteries and sketes,[14] and preached to the fathers dwelling in them, he remained there for some time and read the divine books of the Church Fathers. But being unable to endure any longer the love that burned in his heart for benefiting the Christians — as he himself often said to many of the fathers — he left the Holy Mountain and beginning from the villages outside the Mountain he went and preached at Thessaloniki, Verroia, and nearly all of Macedonia. He proceeded to Himarra, Akarnania, Aitolia, and went as far as Arta and Preveza. From here he sailed to Aghia Mavra[15] and Kephallenia. Wherever the thrice-blessed one went, a large gathering of Christians was formed and they listened with contrition and devoutness to his eloquent and sweet words; and there resulted a great rectification of their deeds and an improvement of their souls.

His teaching, as we have heard it ourselves, was extremely simple, like that of the fishermen.[16] It was so calm and quiet that it seemed generally to be full of the grace of the joyous and quiet Holy Spirit. But God, too, aided and confirmed his words by means of signs and miracles, as He had confirmed through the miracles the preaching of the holy Apostles. Thus, in the island of Kephallenia there was a poor tailor, who for many years had a withered and inactive hand. Now he ran to the Saint and besought to be healed. The Saint urged him to come and listen to his teaching with devoutness, and told him that God would show His compassion. The poor tailor obeyed; and having heard the sermon, behold the miracle! the next day he was healed. Another man, a paralytic, upon hearing of this strange event, had people carry him with his bed to the Saint, at the time when he was preaching. And in a few days he, too, fully recovered his health, and praised God and thanked the Saint. At the fortress of Assos there was a noble who had been suffering from a dreadful disease of the ears, and for many years was almost deaf. This man went with devoutness and faith to the place where the Saint was teaching, and at once began to hear clearly. And from that time on he remained cured.

Because of the large crowds that gathered to hear him, wherever the church could not accommodate them, of necessity he preached outdoors, in the fields. It was his custom, when he was going to stay and preach outdoors, first to ask the people to make a wooden cross for him and set it up there. Then, placing against the cross the footstool which, as they say, had been made for him, like a throne, by Kurt Pasha, he ascended upon it and preached. After his sermon, he separated the footstool into its component parts and took it with him wherever he went, whereas the cross remained there as a perpetual reminder of his teaching. At the places where these crosses were set God worked miracles. For instance, at the center of the marketplace of Argostoli, the main town of Kephallenia, where the Saint left such a cross, there gushed up wonderful water, which can be seen to this day, never having diminished since then.

From Kephallenia he passed over to Zakynthos,[17] accompanied by more than ten caiques full of pious Kephallonites. But he was not well received, and therefore after preaching here only a little he returned to Kephallenia. From here he went to Corfu, where he was received in a grand manner by all and especially by the sovereign of the island. However, as a very large crowd gathered from the villages to

hear the teaching of the Saint, the leaders of the city,
fearing the excitement of ill will, begged him to leave
speedily.[18] Thus, in order not to occasion scandals
and disturbances to the people, he departed from
there and went to the mainland across from Corfu,
that is, to Albania, and here he preached to the
Christians, walking and going through those bar-
baric provinces, where piety and Christian life were
in danger of disappearing completely through the
great ignorance of the Christians there and the many
murders, thefts and other kinds of lawlessness into
which they had fallen, having almost become worse
than the godless. By sowing the seeds of the word
of God in the uncultivated and wild hearts of those
Christians, he produced, with the help of the ac-
tion of Divine grace, many and great fruits. He
tamed the wild, mollified brigands, rendered the
heartless and merciless merciful, the godless godly,
taught those ignorant and uneducated in religion
to attend church services, and in a word caused all
sinners to repent and correct their ways, so that
everybody remarked that a new Apostle had made
his appearance in their time.

Through his teaching he established schools
everywhere, both primary and secondary, not only
in towns but also in villages, in order that children
might go to them and learn sacred letters gratis, and

thereby become firm in the Faith and in piety, and be guided in the virtuous way of life and conduct. He persuaded the wealthy to buy over four thousand large, copper-coated baptismal basins, and dedicated them to churches, so that they may remain there permanently in memory of their donors and that the children of Christians may be baptized in the proper manner.[19] Similarly, he persuaded the well-to-do to buy books by the Church Fathers as well as Christian handbooks, prayer-ropes *(kombologia)*, little crosses, kerchiefs and combs. Of these, the books he distributed to those who could read and to those who promised to learn to read; the kerchiefs (over forty thousand) he distributed to the women, to cover their heads;[20] the combs he gave away to those who vowed to leave their beards[21] and live in a virtuous and Christian manner; while the prayer-ropes and the crosses (over five hundred thousand) he gave away to the common people,[22] asking them to forgive the sins of those who had paid for them.

He had forty to fifty priests who followed him, and when he was about to go from one place to another he sent word to the Christians to confess, fast, and hold a vigil service, lighting many candles. He had specially made wooden stands for the candles, each of which had space for a hundred of them.

ΟΙ ΑΓΙ ΟΣ   ΚΟΣΜΑΣ

ὁ ἰσαπόστολος

ἀντεγράφη
διὰ χειρὸς
Φωτίου Κον=
τογλου
ἀπὸ νά

St. Cosmas Holding a Prayer-rope

Copy, made by Photios Kontogiou in 1951, of a holy icon
in the Church of St. Nicholas in Zitsa, northwestern Greece.

These stands he separated into their parts when he
was ready to leave and took them with him. He
distributed candles gratis to all, and then had priests
read the Holy Unction, and all the Christians were
anointed; and after this he preached. In view of the
fact that large crowds followed him — as many as
two or three thousand — he used to give instructions the night before that many bagfuls of bread
and caldrons of boiled wheat be prepared. These
were taken out to the road where the crowds were
going to pass, and thus everyone partook of them
and forgave the living and the dead.

God worked through him miracles such as the
following, both in Albania and elsewhere:

A certain Turkish officer, incited by the Jews or
by a demon, developed such a hatred against the
Saint that on one occasion he mounted his horse
and dashed forth to overtake the Saint and harm
him. But as the horse was running, it threw the
officer down and crushed his right leg. And when
he returned home he found his son dead. As a con-
sequence he repented and sent a letter to the Saint,
in which he asked to be forgiven.

At Philiates, the leading Agas went to see the
Saint and hear his teaching. As it was summer, they
slept outdoors in a field. During the night, they saw
a heavenly light, like a cloud, which covered the

place where the Saint was staying. They described
this event to the Christians; and in the morning they
asked the Saint to give them his sincere blessing.

Near Phanari, at a place called Lycourisi,[23] a
regional Turkish official, seeing a cross which the
Saint had left there after preaching, as it was his
custom to do, removed it and was bringing it to his
home for the purpose of making two posts for the
bed which he had at his farm. But at once, behold
the miracle! there occurred what seemed to be an
earthquake, and unable to stand on his feet, he fell
down and rolled about gnashing his teeth and
frothing like a demoniac. Then he was lifted by two
Turks who happened to be passing by, and coming to his senses he realized that this happened to
him as a result of Divine wrath, because of his
audacity to remove the holy Cross. Hence, of his
own accord, he took it and placed it where it was
before, and every day thereafter he went there and
kissed it with great devoutness. When the holy
Teacher passed from there on another occasion, the
same Turk went and venerated him, frankly nar-
rated the miracle to all, and humbly asked to be
forgiven.

The Saint censured women that wore ornaments,
and through his teaching persuaded them to give
them all up, to such an extent that some of them

dressed themselves in black. A certain wealthy woman at Koritza had a child, whose head she used to adorn with many sequins and other superfluous ornaments. The Saint often counseled her to give these away to poor children, if she wanted her child to live. But she did not obey. Finally, he told her that if she did not remove these ornaments from her child, she would soon be deprived of it. And since even then she did not heed his counsel, the next day she found her child dead in bed. Then she realized that God had chastised her for her disobedience.

Again, as the Saint taught the Christians, wherever he went, not to buy and sell on Sundays, or do other kinds of work, but to go to church and hear the holy services and the Divine words, those who disobeyed were chastened in various ways. Thus, at a place called Halkiades, about an hour from Arta, a certain traveling vendor who disobeyed and dared to sell goods on Sunday at once suffered paralysis of his hand. He ran to the Saint and asked to be forgiven; and in a few days he was healed. Similarly, at Parga, a certain owner of a workshop wanted to sell something on Sunday, and as a result his hand became stiff. He confessed his sin before the Saint, and after being admonished by him was forgiven and recovered fully the use of his hand.

These and many other miracles were performed

through him by God. We omit them for the sake of brevity.

The Saint had often said openly in his sermons that he had been called to the preaching of the Gospel by Jesus Christ Himself, and that he was going to shed his blood out of his love for Jesus. His prediction was finally fulfilled. The fulfillment took place in the following manner:

This Apostolic Teacher had never opened his mouth to say a word against the Jews, either at Thessaloniki, or at Kastoria, or at Ioannina, or at any other place where there were Jews. He only taught the Christians to live as Christians, and to remain true and faithful to the authorities that God had given them, as the Albanians themselves who used to go and listen to him out in the fields had heard from his mouth, and regarded him as a man of God. To such an extent did they esteem him, that Kurt Pasha, hearing of his good reputation ordered him to appear before him. He liked what he said so much, that he made for him that throne which we mentioned earlier, and covered it with silk, in order that he might go up on it and teach the people from an elevated place. But the very sly and Christ-hating Jews of Ioannina, unable to bear the preaching of the Faith and Gospel of Christ, went and told the Pasha of that region that this holy Cosmas had been sent by the Russians to mislead the royal *rayahs*[24] to go to Russia. However, Divine Providence protected him then from that deadly plot. Henceforth the holy Cosmas stigmatized the slyness and irreconcilable hatred of the Jews towards the Christians. Unable any longer to see and hear the Saint censuring them, the Jews went to Kurt Pasha and gave him a huge sum of money to kill the holy man. Consulting with his Mullah, the Pasha decided to put Cosmas to death through the Mullah.

The execution took place under the following circumstances. The Saint had the custom, wherever he went to preach, first to get the permission of the local Bishop or his trustees; and also to send Christians to get the same permission from the secular authorities, and thus he preached unhindered. Now when he went to an Albanian village named Kolikontasi, he received the permission of the Bishop of that region. Inquiring about the secular authorities and learning that Kurt Pasha governed those regions, and that he lived at a city named Berati, twelve hours away, and learning further that the Mullah of the Pasha lived nearby, he sent a man and procured a permit and preached. However, he was not satisfied, and wanted to go to the Mullah in person for greater assurance. So taking with him four monks and a priest as an interpreter, he went to the Mullah. The latter pretended that he had letters from Kurt Pasha telling him to send Cosmas to him in order that they might converse. Hence he commanded his men to guard the Saint until such time as he should send him to the Pasha, not allowing him to leave the courtyard. The blessed Teacher now realized that they intended to put him to death. Therefore he glorified and thanked the Lord Christ, Who had deemed him worthy of terminating the path of Apostolic teaching with martyrdom. Then, turning to the monks who accompanied him, he uttered the words of the Psalmist: "We went through fire and water; but Thou hast brought us forth to rest."[22] All that night he praised the Lord with Psalms, showing no sign of sorrow whatsoever over his approaching death. Indeed, he appeared very cheerful, as if he were going to joys and revels.

In the morning, he was taken by seven Turkish executioners and mounted on a horse. They pretended that they were going to take him to Kurt Pasha. But when they were about two hours away, they took him to the bank of a large river, dismounted him, and revealed to him the order which they had from Kurt Pasha to put him to death. The Saint received this decision against him with joy; and kneeling, he prayed to God thanking and glorifying Him that he was sacrificing his life because of his love for Him, as his soul had always desired.

ST. COSMAS AITOLOS

Icon with representations from his life, martyrdom, and
afterward. 1829.

Then he rose and blessed the four parts of the world, making the sign of the cross, and gave his benediction for all the Christians that observed his precepts. The executioners then had him sit down by a tree, and wanted to tie his hands; but the Saint did not let them, saying that he would not resist but would keep his hands crossed, as if they had tied them. Then he leaned his holy head against the tree, and the barbarians tied him around the neck with a rope. As soon as they tightened it, his divine spirit flew to Heaven.

Thus the thrice-blessed Cosmas, that great benefactor of men, became worthy of receiving, at the age of sixty-five, a double crown from the Lord, one as a Peer of the Apostles and the other as a holy Martyr.

His holy body, having been stripped of the clothing by the executioners, was dragged by them and cast into the river with a large stone tied to the neck. Upon learning this, the Christians ran at once to get it out. But after searching with nets and other means they failed to find it. Three days later a devout priest named Father Markos, of the Monastery of the Presentation of the Most Holy Theotokos near the village of Kolikontasi, went into a canoe, crossed himself, and set out in search of the the body. Presently, behold the miracle! He saw the holy body floating in the water upright, as if it were alive. He hastened to it, embraced it, and pulled it out of the water. As he lifted it, a great deal of blood ran out of the mellifluous mouth of the Saint into the river. He covered the body with his cassock and brought it to the above mentioned Monastery of the Theotokos, and buried it honorably behind the sanctuary of the church.

After the death of the Saint, the following events took place. Kurt Pasha repented for having been fooled and put to death such an innocent and peaceful man for empty gain. Therefore he sent a message to his Mullah to let the monks of the Saint, whom he kept under guard, go to the above mentioned Monastery of the Theotokos and stay there. When they arrived there, they found the holy body interred; and in order to learn more about the nature of the martyrdom they exhumed it with the assistance of other priests and lay Christians. Despite the fact that it had been in the river for three days, like Jonah in the belly of the whale, it had not undergone any change and had no offensive odor, but all of it smelled sweetly and seemed to be asleep. After kissing it piously, they buried it again at the same place. Here a divine church was later built in his honor.

The circumstances of the erection of the church

were as follows. During one of his journeys in Albania, in the region of Tepeleni, the Saint had met the Vizir Ali Pasha of Tepeleni, who at that time was still only a Bey, and in fact was being persecuted even by Kurt Pasha. When they met, the Saint told him that the district which he governed would grow a great deal, and that he himself would become a great sovereign, renowned in the world; that he would conquer many cities and all of Albania, and that after a time he would conquer even the stronghold of Kurt Pasha. After some thirty years the prophecies of the Saint were fulfilled. Ali Pasha, having grown tremendously in power, entered the very stronghold of Kurt Pasha, in accordance with prophecy of the Saint. When he entered Berati,[26] the Vizir Ali Pasha remembered the words of the Saint, and calling the bishop of Velegrada[27] ordered him to remove the remains of the Saint from the tomb and build a monastery dedicated to the Saint, because he had known him as a true man of God through his prophecy and other things. So after some time, the remains of the Saint were removed, and his venerable head was at once covered with silver at the order of his highness, the Sovereign Vizir Ali Pasha. Immediately after this, Ali Pasha ordered that contributions be gathered from the public; and the famous church which is dedicated to the Saint was erected. Such

was the way in which this divine church was built
from the foundations, through the contribution and
exhortation and high command of the most mighty
and most high Vizir Ali Pasha of Tepeleni, at the
time when Joasaph was Archbishop of Velegrada.

ON GOD

In one of his *Didachai,* as his sermons came to be
known, St. Cosmas Aitolos says: "It is proper and
reasonable, as we learn from the Holy Gospels and
the other Divine Scriptures, to begin our teaching
with God; and when we finish, to thank God."[1] St.
Cosmas abided by this counsel. In all of his *Didachai*
he begins by speaking of God, and ends with some
reference to Him. Needless to say, he does not
dispense with God in the parts of the *Didachai* between the beginning and the end. Like all true
saints, he had his mind continuously turned towards
God; and so he refers to God throughout his eight
sermons that have come down to us, and also in
his personal letters. He speaks of the Holy Trinity,
and of the three Persons that constitute it. He mentions many attributes of God, and speaks of God's
relation to man and of man's relation to him. What
Aitolos says is of great interest as a clear and simple exposition of the teaching of the Orthodox

49

Ὁ Ἅγιος ΚΟCΜΑC ὁ νέος

ST. COSMAS THE NEW,
THE AITOLIAN

Drawing inspired by an old icon.

Church about God, as an example of an ardent espousal of this teaching by a great saint of the Church who lived in the eighteenth century, and as an underscoring of certain attributes of God that is characteristic of the Orthodox conception of the Deity.

Our Saint often mentions both metaphysical and moral attributes. Among the metaphysical attributes cited are unity in trinity, omnipotence, light, life, and creativity; among the moral, goodness, compassion, mercifulness, justice, and love.

Regarding the *unity* of God, Cosmas remarks: "God is one and whoever says that there are many gods is a devil."[2] Again, he says: "God is one nature, one glory, one kingdom, one God."[3]

He frequently speaks of God as the "Holy Trinity" or the "All-Holy Trinity," and mentions the three Persons constituting it: the Father, the Son, and the Holy Spirit. Although he notes that the Trinity is a mystery, being incomprehensible and inexplicable,[3] he on two occasions gives illustrations of the relationships between the three Persons. He observes that we do not have any example with which to compare the Holy Trinity, because there exists none in the world; yet he goes on to add that the theologians of the Church, in order to offer a slight

help to our mind, give some examples. One such
example is, he says, this:

"The sun is, as we all know, one, and God is one;
and just as the sun illuminates this sensible world,
so the Holy Trinity illuminates the intelligible
world. We said that the sun is one, but it is also
three: it has rays which come to our eyes like lines,
like threads; and it has light which spreads to the
whole world. To the sun we liken the eternal Father;
to the rays, the coeternal Son; and to the light, the
consubstantial Spirit."[5]

Another illustration which the blessed Cosmas cites
is taken not from the external, physical world, but
from the internal world, from the human soul and
its powers. He says:

"The soul is one; a person begets the power of
discursive reason; then there is also breath, which
belongs to the soul, not to the body. The soul is com-
parable with the Father; discursive reason, with the
Son and Logos of God; the breath of the soul, with
the All-Holy Spirit. The soul begets discursive
reason *(logos)* through intuitive reason *(nous),* and
secondly, discursive reason is begotten by the lips.
And just as discursive reason is first begotten by the
soul, and is not manifested, and then by means of
the lips becomes manifest, so the Son and Logos
of God was begotten before all ages by God the

Father. But He was not made manifest to mankind, but abided in the bosom of the Father. Secondly, He was begotten from the lips of the Prophets and the all-pure and Ever-Virgin Mary, and became manifest to the whole world."[6]

St. Cosmas adds that there is another, better way of understanding the Holy Trinity: through the illumination of Divine grace. Such illumination, he remarks, will come to us if we confess candidly and receive Holy Communion with fear and devoutness.[7]

Omnipotence, while ascribed to the Holy Trinity, is not dwelt upon. The Saint simply asserts that God is omnipotent.[8]

The attribute of *light* is given more emphasis. Our Saint speaks of the Holy Trinity as "one glory," as "all light," and as "illuminating the intelligible world."[9] By "intelligible world" *(noetos kosmos)* he means the world of angels and of human souls. The illuminating activity of God is dwelt upon in connection with the Holy Spirit, of Whom I shall speak later. The grace of the Holy Spirit, Aitolos asserts, illumined the Prophets, the Apostles, and the Fathers of the Church, and illumines all those who lead a pious Christian life, praying regularly, confessing and receiving Holy Communion.

Like the attribute of omnipotence, that of *life* is

not discussed.[10] It is clear, however, that Cosmas does not have at all in mind the biological notion of life, but a purely spiritual one.

The *creativity* of God is referred to more often than His omnipotence and life, and is explained. Although the Saint does not employ the term "creativity," he refers to God as "Creator," and asserts that He created "heaven and earth," that is, "the whole intelligible and sensible world."[11]

Turning to the moral attributes of God, we note that the most often mentioned one is *goodness*. There are innumerable statements in the *Didachai* in which God is said to be "all-good."[12] St. Cosmas sees the goodness of God conspicuously in the creation of the physical world *for our sake.* Thus, he remarks:

"God gave us such a great earth in order that we may dwell here temporarily; He gave us so many thousands of plants, fountains, rivers, seas, air, day and night, the sky, the sun, and so on. For whom did He make all these except us? What did He owe us? Nothing. All these are a gift."[13]

Cosmas also sees the goodness in the goal for which He created us. "God," he says, "did not create us for the devil and for hell, but for Himself and for Paradise."[14]

Intimately related to His goodness are the other moral attributes that were mentioned earlier: *com-*

passion, mercifulness, justice, and *love.* God, the Holy Trinity, is asserted to be "compassionate"[15] and "all compassion."[16] He is said to be "very merciful,"[17] and at the same time just.[18] St. Cosmas emphasizes the justice of God. Thus, he says: "God is compassionate, but He is also just. He has an iron rod: He chastised Adam and Eve. Similarly He chastises us also, if we do not act rightly. Adam and Eve transgressed the commandment of God, and they were exiled from Paradise."[19]

The Aitolian saint places special emphasis on the attribute of love. Thus, he says: "Our all-good and very merciful God, my brethren, has many and different names: He is called light and life, and resurrection; however, the chief name of our God is and is said to be love."[20]

Having spoken of the Holy Trinity taken in its unity, let us now turn to the three Persons of the Trinity, and see what the divine Cosmas says about each of them. About the Father, he does not say very much. The Father is always mentioned first, when the three Persons of the Trinity are listed, the Son being mentioned next, and then the Holy Spirit.[21] We have already seen this in the two illustrations of the Holy Trinity. In the second illustration, we saw how the Father is said to be the timeless begetter of the second Person of the Trinity, the Son

and Logos. The Father is also spoken of as eternal
and "almighty."[23] These attributes He has in common with the other two Persons.

About the second Person, Aitolos has much more
to say. He speaks of Him as "perfect God and perfect
man,"[24] as "the Son and Logos of God and true
God,"[25] as "Son of man,"[26] as coeternal with the
Father,[27] as the creator of the whole world, intelligible and sensible,[28] as the life of all,[29] as wisdom,[30]
as the only teacher.[31] Especially characteristic of his
references to Christ is the adjective "sweetest." He
often speaks of Christ as "our sweetest Master" or
"our sweetest Jesus Christ and God."[32] This appella-
tion evinces the profound love which he had for
Jesus Christ, viewed as all-good, compassionate,
humble and meek, in accordance with our Lord's
own statement: "Take my yoke upon you, and learn
of me; for I am meek and humble in heart: and ye
shall find rest unto your souls. For my yoke is easy,
and my burden is light."[33] The expression may be
taken also to evince the spiritual joy which he experienced as he invoked Jesus in his practice of the
Jesus Prayer, to which he refers several times in his
Didachai. His younger contemporary St. Nicodemos
the Hagiorite, who also practiced this prayer, says
in his *Handbook of Counsel:* "You will experience in-
effable joy if you should come to love and practice

mental prayer, or prayer of the heart, unceasingly remembering the sweetest name, the joy-giving and most beautiful giver of light, Jesus."[34]

The Incarnation of Christ, His being born as a man by "our Lady Theotokos and Ever-Virgin Mary," is, remarks the blessed Cosmas, a result of His great goodness towards mankind.[35] Christ "condescended," he says, "and became perfect man by the Holy Spirit and from the purest blood of the Theotokos, in order that we might escape from the hands of the devil and become sons and heirs of His kingdom, to rejoice forever in Paradise together with the angels, and not to burn in hell with the impious and the demons."[36]

The third Person of the Trinity, the Holy Spirit, is declared to be consubstantial with the Father and the Son.[37] His importance in relation to man lies particularly in the fact that He illumined the Prophets, the Apostles, and the Fathers of the Church to write for us."[38] Elsewhere, being more specific, he says: "The Holy Spirit illumined firstly the holy Prophets, and they wrote for us the sacred Scriptures. Secondly, He illumined the holy Apostles. And thirdly, He illumined the holy Fathers, and they explained the books of our Church, in order that we may know how to conduct ourselves."[39] As an example of the Prophets, the divine Cosmas cites

Moses. He quotes the opening sentence in the book
of Genesis: "In the beginning God created heaven
and earth," and remarks that Moses made this statement, and those that follow, "illuminated by the
Holy Spirit."[40] In connection with the Apostles, he
observes that besides illuminating them, the Holy
Spirit conferred upon them the gift of healing. With
the grace which they received from the Spirit, "they
healed the blind, the deaf, the lepers, those possessed
by demons."[41] With regard to the faithful in general,
he notes the efficacy of Holy Communion in drawing to them illuminating Divine grace. The Holy
Eucharist, he says, when preceded by candid repentance and approached with fear and reverence, "illuminates one and renders him like an angel."[42]

In presenting the Orthodox doctrine of God in
his *Didachai,* St. Cosmas was not concerned with
the mere transmission of theological knowledge, but
rather with helping people transform themselves and
their lives by utilizing this knowledge. It is essential that one have a true conception of the Deity;
but this conception should not be taken as mere
information to be stored in memory as dead
academic knowledge: it should be consciously enter-
tained. Thus, the Saint remarks: "Whoever has his
mind on God is rendered worthy by him of living
well here and of going to Paradise."[43] He tells his

listeners much about Christ, because he regards knowledge of Christ as of great value for us. Thus, he observes: "In our Lord Jesus Christ is seen the Holy Trinity,"[44] and again, "in the prayer 'Lord Jesus Christ,. . . have mercy upon me, a sinner,' what does one see? One sees the Holy Trinity, our God, the incarnate dispensation of our Christ."[45] These statements are in accord with what Christ Himself says in the Gospel according to John: "I am the way, the truth, and the life; no man cometh unto the Father, but by me. If ye had known me, ye should also have known my Father; and henceforth ye know him, and have seen him."[46] Orthodox theologians explain that we know God the Father in Christ through the grace we receive from the Holy Spirit. As grace is drawn to us most effectively through continual prayer, especially mental prayer or prayer of the heart, St. Cosmas takes the opportunity to urge his audiences to practice the Jesus Prayer, saying mentally: "Lord Jesus Christ, Son and Logos of the living God, through the intercessions of the Theotokos and all the saints, have mercy upon me, Thy sinful and unworthy servant."[47] This is a longer form of the Jesus Prayer, the shorter form, recommended by the ascetic-mystical Fathers whose texts are included in the *Philokalia,* being: "Lord Jesus Christ, Son of God, have mercy upon me."

Through this prayer, remarks Cosmas, we not only come into relation with the Holy Trinity, receive Divine grace, experience God, but we also make progress towards our ultimate goal, which is to attain salvation, to "go to Paradise."[48] "With the cross and the prayer 'Lord Jesus Christ,'" he says, "all the saints went to Paradise." He adds that through the cross and the Jesus Prayer "all diseases are cured."[49]

St. Cosmas does not content himself with mentioning the attributes of God, but takes every opportunity to indicate their relevance to us. Thus, he not only says that God is very merciful, but remarks that God manifests His mercifulness when we sin: He does not cause us to die and go to hell, but waits for us to repent, to stop doing evil and do good, to confess and correct ourselves, so that He may embrace us and put us in Paradise, to rejoice forever.[50]

In speaking about the goodness and love of God, our Saint likewise takes the opportunity to point out the relevance of this divine attribute to us. Thus, he says that it is our duty to love God and do His commandments, because God, out of his goodness and love for us, has given us this great earth to dwell on and has made provision for all our needs.[51] He also notes that our Lord Jesus Christ shed His blood for us, and hence we in return ought to love God and if need be shed our blood for Him.[52] This, he notes, is precisely what Prophets, Apostles, and countless Martyrs have done. "They shed their blood out of their love for the Holy Trinity, and they attained Paradise and rejoice forever."[53]

In connection with God's love for us, the blessed Cosmas observes that God loves the humble; and in the light of this he urges his listeners to avoid pride and to cultivate the virtue of humility.[54]

One could cite other examples of the Saint's endeavor to make the Orthodox view of God relevant to the everyday life of men. But these should suffice.

The message of St. Cosmas to his fellow Christians regarding their proper relation to God could be summed up in these few words: Orient yourselves decisively towards God. Keep your mind and aspirations turned to Him.[55] Abide in the Orthodox Christian faith.[56] Fulfill the Divine commandments.[57]Pray to God as often as possible to have mercy upon you. Glorify and worship daily the Father, the Son, and the Holy Spirit.[58]

ON HEAVEN AND HELL

Like the subject of God, that of heaven and hell is central in St. Cosmas' teaching. We have noted that his sermons begin and end with reference to God, and repeatedly refer to Him. They also begin and end with reference to heaven and hell, and frequently touch this topic. He begins by speaking of the Incarnation of the second Person of the Holy Trinity as having as its purpose to help man attain salvation *(soteria)*. Salvation means escaping hell *kolasis)* and attaining paradise *(paradeisos)* or the kingdom of heaven *(basileia ton ouranon)*. Cosmas puts the matter thus at the beginning of the first *Didache:*

"Our Lord and God Jesus Christ, my brethren, our sweetest master, the creator of the angels and of the whole intelligible and sensible world, moved by His great goodness, which He has for mankind, together with the infinite gifts which He has given us and bestows upon us every day, hour and moment, condescended and became perfect man of the Holy Spirit and of the most pure blood of our Lady

Theotokos and Ever-Virgin Mary, in order to make us escape from the hands of the devil and render us sons and heirs of His kingdom, to rejoice forever in paradise together with the angels, and not burn in hell with the impious and the devils."[1]

Father Cosmas proceeds to indicate to his listeners the means they should adopt if they want to be saved, to attain paradise, and the ways they should avoid, as leading to perdition, to hell.

Typically, his sermons end with a prayer that God render his brethren worthy of faring well in this life and going to paradise after death. Thus, at the end of the first *Didache* he says:

"May God have compassion on you and forgive your sins, and render you worthy of faring well and living peacefully in this vain life, and of going after death to paradise, our true fatherland and rejoicing forever, glorifying and worshipping the Holy Trinity unto the ages of ages. Amen."[2]

What heaven or paradise is, and *what* hell is, our Saint does not undertake to discuss. He confines himself to speaking of heaven as a place and state of unending, eternal joy and delight, in the company of the holy angels and saints, and hell as a place and state of everlasting burning, of suffering, together with the demons and the sinners — the impious, heretics, unbelievers, atheists.

He says a great deal, however, about the *works* that lead to heaven and those that lead to hell. By works *(erga)* he means not only overt acts, but also settled dispositions of the soul, thoughts, and feelings. About works in general, he remarks in one of his *Didachai:*

"The soul will rejoice forever in paradise if it does good works, but it will burn in hell if it does evil ones."[3]

In another sermon he says:

"How are Christians saved? Each one fares according to how he has acted. That is, if he has done good works, he goes to paradise, if evil ones, he goes to hell."[4]

What he means by "good works" and "evil works" can easily be gathered from what he says in his sermons. "Good works" consist of the whole Christian way of life. Cosmas emphassizes particularly the virtues of *faith, humility, love, almsgiving, forgiveness, justice, temperance, virginity,* the practices of *repentance, confession, receiving Holy Communion, fasting, prayer —* both *private* and *corporate —*, and in general *keeping the Divine commandments.* "Evil works" consist of the opposites of these; *lack of faith* or *unbelief, pride, hatred, indifference to the needy, unforgiveness, injustice, incontinence, fornication, unrepentance, not confessing, not communing, not fasting, not praying,* and in general *not observing the Divine commandments.*

Stressing the importance of *faith (pistis)*, which is the beginning and constant presupposition of the Christian way of life, Cosmas says that at the Second Coming, Christ will declare to the righteous: "Come, ye blessed of my Father, inherit paradise, to rejoice forever together with my angels, for ye kept my faith and my commandments;" while to the sinners He will say: "Depart ye accursed ones into hell, to burn forever together with the devil, your father, for ye did not keep my faith and my commandents."[5]

About faith, he also makes this statement:

"Our Lord Jesus Christ, the true God, sent the twelve Apostles to the whole world, telling them: Go everywhere, to the whole earth, to fortresses and villages, and tell people, if perhaps they want to live well and peacefully here, and to be put by me into paradise, they must believe and be baptized in the name of the Father and of the Son and of the Holy Spirit, and must keep the commandments of the Holy Gospels."[6]

Concerning *humility (tapeinosis)* and its relation to paradise, there this remarkable passage in the first *Didache:*

"Let us flee from pride, my brethren, for it is the first daughter of the devil, it is a path that leads to hell. Let us have instead humility, for it is angelic, is a path that leads us to paradise. . ."[7]

A great deal is said by Aitolos about *spiritual love (agape)*, the highest of the Christian virtues, in its relation to salvation, to attaining heaven. The following are some characteristic passages:

"Let us have love for God and for our brethren. Then comes our God and gives us joy, and plants in our heart the eternal life, and we fare well here and go to paradise to rejoice forever,"[8]

"Even if we should do a thousand of thousands good deeds, my brethren — fasts, prayers, almsgiving — , even if we should shed our blood for our Christ, but do not have these two loves, but have hatred and enmity towards our brethren, all these good acts which we have performed are the devil's and we go to hell."[9]

"Our love must be true. With pseudo love we do not go to paradise.[10]

"We must love our enemies and forgive them; we must offer them food and drink; we must entreat God in behalf of their soul, and then say to God: 'My God, I beg you to forgive me, as I forgive my enemies.' If, however, we do not forgive our enemies, even if we should shed our blood for the love of Christ, we go to hell."[11]

"If you want God to forgive all your sins and write

you down for paradise, say for your enemies three times: May God forgive them and have mercy upon them."[12]

St. Cosmas puts much emphasis on *almsgiving (eleemosyne),* which is a form of love. Thus, he says that almsgiving sanctifies man.[13] As illustrations of this, he cites king Manasses, and Abraham and Sarah. About Manasses he relates the following:

"In ancient times there was a king of the Hebrews named Manasses, who tortured them with many kinds of punishment. The prophets and teachers advised him to rule the people with gentleness; but he did no listen to the word of God, did not repent. Seeing his evil state of mind, what does God do? He rouses a king from the east that wages war against him, captures him a slave, and locks him up in a caldron to burn him. What does Manasses do there, inside the copper caldron? He remembers his sins, weeps, and entreats God to free him and promises to sin no more. Seeing his good state of mind, God listened to his repentance, accepted his tears, and sent an angel who liberated him from that danger. Then Manasses sold his possessions and gave them away as alms, and went and led an ascetic life during his remaining years, with fasts, vigils, and prayers. And he went to paradise to rejoice forever."[14]

Reference to *forgiveness (synchoresis)* as leading to Paradise has already been made in connection with love. Forgiveness is an expression of love for our fellow men.

With regard to *justice* as essential for salvation, St. Cosmas says:

"My brethren, those of you who have done injustice to Christians, or Jews, or Turks, give back what you deprived them of, because it is cursed and you make no progress. You eat what you acquired unjustly in order to live, and this kills you and God puts you in hell."[15]

Regarding *temperance (sophrosyne)* and *virginity (parthenia)* our Saint remarks:

"Men and women lived in the world with temperance and virginity, ... and they fared well here and went to paradise to rejoice forever."[16]

Concerning *repentance (matanoia)* he says:

"Our all-good and very merciful God, my brethren, . . . even if we sin a thousand times an hour, has compassion on us as a father and does not cause us to die, to put us in hell, but waits with open arms for our repentance, for the time when we will repent, will stop doing evil and will do what is good, will confess, will correct ourselves, in order to embrace us and put us in Paradise to rejoice forever."[17]

Confession (exomologesis) is duly emphasized. The divine Cosmas says:

"And if you want me, my children, to tell you, go and find a spiritual father, one who is practical and a man of virtue, and confess to him, tell him your sins. Do not leave any unconfessed, for if you do, you lose all your reward."[18]

"You ought to confess every day, if you can, but if you cannot confess every day, let it be once a week or once a month, or at the very least four times a year. And accustom your children from an early age in the good path, to confess."[19]

Stressing the value of *Holy Communion (Achranta Mysteria)* for attaining Paradise, Cosmas remarks:

"The eleven Apostles, as soon a they received the Immaculate Mysteria with a good mental disposition, with good will, were illuminated, brightened, became wise teachers of the world, and with that joy they spoke all the languages of the world; and they fared well here and went to Paradise to rejoice forever.[20]

"If we, too, wish to benefit by the Immaculate Mysteria like the eleven Apostles, the good ones, and not to be harmed like evil Judas, we should confess candidly and receive Holy Communion with trembling and devoutness, and then we shall be illumined. But if we go without confession, defiled with sins, and dare to receive the Immaculate Mysteria, we put fire inside us and burn."[21]

Noting the value of *fasting (nesteia),* Aitolos says:

"Moses fasted for forty days and forty nights, and he became like an angel. . . .[22] We pious Christians, too, must fast always, but especially on Wednesday, because the Lord was sold on that day, and on Friday, because He was crucified on that day. Similarly, we ought to fast also during the Lents, as the Holy Spirit illumined the holy Fathers of the Church and they ordained that we fast in order to mortify the passions and humble the body, and because eating less makes living easier. . . Do you keep the four Lents, my Christians? If you are Christians, you must keep them especially the Great Lent."[23]

"Almsgiving, love, and fasting sanctify man, enrich him in body and soul, and he has a good end."[24]

Great importance is assigned by St. Cosmas to *prayer (proseuche),* especially *mental prayer (noera proseuche).* He gives this advice regarding the practice of mental prayer:

"Now I advise you to take a prayer-rope *(kombologi),* young and old, and hold it in your left hand, and with your right hand cross yourselves and say:

'Lord Jesus Christ, Son and Logos of the living God, by the intercessions of the Theotokos and all the Saints, have mercy upon me the sinner and unworthy servant of Thee.' With the cross let us open Paradise, with the cross let us drive away demons. But we must have our hand clean of sins, and then the devil is burned and flees. Wherefore, my brethren, whether you eat, or drink, or work, let not this prayer and the cross be absent from you. It is good and holy to pray always at dawn, in the evening, and at midnight."[25]

Giving more specific instructions, he counsels:

"All of you, take a prayer-rope, which should have one hundred and three knots. At every knot say: 'Lord Jesus Christ, Son and Logos of the living God, by the intercessions of the Theotokos and all the Saints have mercy upon me the sinner and unworthy servant of Thee."[26]

And he adds:

"By means of the cross and 'Lord Jesus Christ' man is sanctified and goes to Paradise, to rejoice and delight like the angels."[26]

Besides private prayer, the Saint exhorts people to participate in corporate prayer, worship in church:

"Do not separate yourselves from Christ and from the Church. Do you hear the priest sounding the bells? At once rise, wash yourselves, and go to church, to listen to the Orthros with attention. Similarly, attend the Divine Liturgy. And counsel your children, as much as you can, not to sin, to go to church, to be blessed, in order to live and progress. Whoever, my brethren, hears the bells and is slothful to go to church shall be drowned by sin, as people were drowned at the Deluge. . . The priest is a herald of the ark. The church is an ark. Those brethren who worship in church will be forgiven their sins, and they will not be drowned by their faults."[28]

Indicating briefly *ways* through which we may avoid hell and attain Paradise, he cites (1) the way of Martyrdom, (2) the way of Monasticism, and (3) the way of the Righteous in the world. About the first way he remarks:

"Prophets, Apostles, Martyrs and Ascetics spilt their blood for their love of the Holy Trinity, and they bought Paradise and rejoice forever."[29]

About the second way he says:

"Men and women renounced the world, went to the desert and led an ascetic life during the remainder of their days, and they went to Paradise."[30]

And concerning the third way he says this:

"Also, men and women lived in the world with temperance and virginity, with fasts, prayers, almsgiving, with good works, and they fared well here and went to Paradise and rejoice forèver."[31]

Concluding his teaching on heaven and hell, St. Cosmas admonishes:

"Therefore, my brethren, let us reflect what we are, righteous or sinners. If we are righteous, we are fortunate and thrice-blessed; but if we are sinners, we ought to repent now that we have time, giving up evil and doing good. Hell awaits us; when will we repent? Not tomorrow, or the day after tomorrow, or next year, but this hour. For we do not know what will happen to us until tomorrow. Christ tells us to be always ready."[32]

PROPHECIES OF THE SAINT

St. Cosmas Aitolos received from God the gift of prophecy. He foretold many events that subsequently did in fact take place. His prophecies are many. The late Father Haralambos Vasilopoulos lists ninety-nine prophecies in his book on St. Cosmas,[1] while Metropolitan Augustine Kantiotis and Markos Giolias list one hundred twenty-five.[2] Most of the prophecies have already been fulfilled. The majority, pertain to the liberation of the Greeks from Turkish rule. Several have reference to inventions such as the automobile, the airplane, the telephone, and satellites.

I have selected sixteen of the prophecies — those which are of wider interest — from Kantiotis' book and present them below together with some comments.

1. "This will one day become Greek *(Romaiiko)*, and fortunate will be whoever will live in that kingdom." (St. Cosmas used to say this of various parts of Greece that were under Turkish rule and were later liberated.)

2. "That which is longed for will take place in the third generation. It will be seen by your grandchildren." (Metropolitan Augustine Kantiotis remarks: "This exceedingly important prophecy of the Saint, which nursed the sweetest hope of the enslaved Greek people, received astonishing fulfillment. For the years of the liberation of the Nation are in fact the third generation from the time when the Saint made this prophecy, inasmuch, as is known, each generation is reckoned as twenty-five years."[3])

3. "There will come the red caps, and afterwards the English for fifty-four years, and then this region will become Greek *(Romaiiko)*." (This was said in the island of Kephallenia (Cephalonia) regarding the liberation of the Heptanese, also known as the Ionian Islands, which were under Venetian occupation. Kantiotis says this about the prophecy: "The French soldiers were called 'red caps,' because their headgear was red during the years of Napoleon. This prophecy found amazing fulfillment. For after the Venetians, the Ionian Islands were taken over

by the French, and after their departure there came the English, whose occupation of them lasted for fifty-four years, that is, as many as the Saint had prophesied. The English seized the Heptanese in 1810 — except for Kerkyra or Corfu, which surrendered in 1815 to Campbell — and in 1864 they gave it up to Greece."[4])

4. "That which is longed for will come when two *Paschalies* will occur together." (The word *Paschalies* — from Pascha, Easter — denotes Easter Sunday and also any other great holy feast. Now in 1912, when Easter and the feast of the Annunciation happened to be on the same day, Epiros and other regions of Greece were liberated from the Turks.)

5. "The Turks will leave, but they shall come again and will arrive as far as Hexamilia. In the end, they shall be driven away to Kokkine Melia. Of the Turks, one third will be killed, another third will be baptized, and the remaining third will go to Kokkine Melia." ("Kokkine Melia was a region which the imagination of the enslaved Greeks placed in the depths of Asia Minor." — Kantiotis.[5])

6. The time will come when the world will be directed by speechless *(alala)* and lifeless *(balala)* things. (This prophecy foretells the invention and use of various machines, especially computers, which have come to dominate the life of mankind.)

7. "The evil will come to you from the learned." (It was by the intelligentsia that atheistic, materilistic, anti-Christian, soul-corrupting ideas have been introduced into Greece from western Europe.)

8. "After the war, men will run half an hour to find another human being to join him in fellowship." (The situation prophesied here fits with that anticipated today in the case of nuclear war.)

9. "The time will come when the devil will make his turns with his pumpkin." ("A strange prophecy! Is it about the technical satellites, which like pumpkins turn about in space and evoke the astonishment of men, who gape before these pumpkins and deify science? By this, we do not wish to depreciate the value of scientific discoveries, but we censure the arrogance of the contemporary world, which seeks to place the idols of the inventions in the place of the true God. In comparison with the enormous spheres which the omnipotence of God has created and released, in order that they might whirl in the vast space, what are the greatly admired technical satellites but small and fragile pumpkins in the infinite universe?" — Kantiotis.[6])

10. "This child will progress, will rule Greece, and will be glorified." (This was said of Ioannes Koletis. In his book *National-martyr Clerics and Father Cosmas,* Lampros K. Kataphygiotis gives the

following account regarding this prophecy: "When he was passing from Syrrako in 1778, Cosmas received hospitality from the wealthy Koletis family, which had a child of about five years of age. This child, charming in every respect, sat in the lap of Cosmas and fondled his beard. The mother of the child had heard about Cosmas' gift of prophecy, and asked him about the future of her child. Cosmas said: 'The child will be educated. He will go abroad. He will become a famous man. And he will die ruler of Greece.' The child was John Koletis, who was born in Syrrako in 1773. He was educated. He went to Europe and became a Physician. He took part in the Revolution of 1821. He became Minister, and in 1847, during the reign of Otto, he died as Prime Minister of Greece."[7])

11. "You will become a great man, you will conquer all of Albania, you will subjugate Preveza, Parga, Souli, Delvino,, Gardiki, and the very stronghold of Kurt Pasha. You will leave a great name in the world. Also, you will go to Constantinople, . . . but with a red beard. This is the will of Divine Providence. Remember, however, throughout your whole reign, to love and defend the Christians, if you want your successors to retain their power." (This was said at Tepeleni, in present day Albania, to Ali Pasha, and found amazing

fulfillment after some thirty years. He became the sole, powerful ruler of Epiros. In saying that Ali Pasha would go to Constantinople but with a "red beard," the Saint meant that Ali Pasha would be beheaded and his head with bloody beard would be sent to that city. This, too, found fulfillment.)

12. "Things will come out of the schools that your mind does not even imagine."

13. "You will see in the field a carriage without horses, running faster than a rabbit."

14. "A time will come when the earth will be girded by a thread."

15. "A time will come when people will speak from one distant place to another, as though they were in adjoining rooms — for example, from Constantinople to Russia."

16. "You will see men flying in the sky like starlings, and throwing fire on the earth. Those who will live then will run to graves and will cry out: 'Come out you who are dead so that we the living may enter.' " ("These five successive prophecies of the Saint evidently have reference to the great inventions of our time. The carriages without horses are the trains and the automobiles. The thread which will encircle the whole world are the telegraph wires. By means of the devices of communication at a distance, the voice is heard from a distance of thou-

sands of kilometers as if it came from the adjacent house. The starlings, which will drop fire on the earth, are the airplanes of the military air forces. These prophecies of Saint Cosmas are in books that were written . . . about a century before the related inventions were made. Hence, they arouse admiration and manifestly testify to the Saint's gift of prophecy." — Kantiotis.[8])

SELECTED PASSAGES FROM
THE *TEACHINGS* OF ST. COSMAS

God

It is proper to begin our teaching with God, and when we finish it to thank God — not that I am worthy to mention and utter the name of God, but I am sure that God suffers me to do so through His great and infinite compassion.[1]

* * *

God, the all-good and most merciful, my brethren, is one, and whoever says that there are many Gods is a devil. He is triune: Father, Son, and Holy Spirit; yet one nature, one glory, one kingdom, one God. He is all light, all joy, all compassion, all love.[2]

* * *

This All-holy Trinity we pious Orthodox Christians glorify and worship. He is the true God, and all other so-called gods are demons. And it is not we alone that believe, glorify, and worship the Holy Trinity, but angels, archangels, and all the heavenly hosts, as numerous as the stars of the heavens and the grains of the sand of the sea unceasingly praise in hymns and worship and glorify this All-holy Trinity. Again, out of their love for the Holy Trinity men and women as numerous as the stars of the heavens and the grains of the sand of the sea spilt their blood, and as many renounced the world and went to the deserts and led a life of spiritual endeavor, and still as many lived in the world with temperance and virginity, fasting, prayer, almsgiving and other practices; and all went to Paradise and rejoice forever.[3]

Love

If we want to fare well in this life and to go to Paradise, and to call our God love and father, we must have two loves: the love for God and the love for our neighbor. It is natural for us to have these two loves, and contrary to nature not have them. Just as a swallow needs two wings in order to fly in the air, so we need these two loves, because without them we cannot be saved.[4]

*   *   *

Let us have love for God and for our fellow men. Then God comes and brings us joy and implants the eternal life in our hearts, and we fare well in this life and also go to Paradise, there to rejoice forever.[5]

*   *   *

Fortunate is the man who has these two loves in his heart, that for God and that for his brethren. He surely has God; and whoever has God has every blessing and does not bear to commit sin. Again, wretched is the man who does not have these two loves. Surely he has the devil and evil, and always sins. God, my brethren, asks us to have these two loves. As He Himself says in His Holy Gospel: "On these two commandments hang all the law and the Prophets."[6] Through these two loves all the Saints of our Church, men and women, attained sainthood and won Paradise.[7]

*   *   *

Whoever has blessed love, firstly for God and secondly for his fellow Christian, becomes worthy of receiving the Holy Trinity in his heart.[8]

*   *   *

If you wish to be saved, seek no other thing here in this world as much as love.[9]

*   *   *

Know my brethren that love has two characteristics, two gifts. One of them is to strengthen man in what is good and the other is to weaken him in what is evil. I have a loaf of bread to eat; you do not have. Love tells me: Do not eat it alone, give some to your brethren and you eat the rest. I have clothes; love tells me: Give one garment to your brother and you wear the other one. I open my mouth to accuse you, to tell you lies, to deceive you; but at once I remember love and it deadens my mouth, and does not allow me to tell you lies. I stretch out my hands to take what belongs to you, your money, all your possessions. Love does not allow me to take them. Do you see, my brethren, what gifts love has?[10]

*   *   *

Those of you who earn your bread by means of your toil and sweat should rejoice, because that bread is blessed; and if you give a little of it as alms it is reckoned as much. But those who live by means of injustice and grasping should mourn, for what you thus acquire is cursed; and if you give alms out of these they do not benefit you at all, being fire that consumes you.[11]

*   *   *

The Martyrs won Paradise through their blood; the Ascetics, through their ascetic life. Now you, my brethren, who have children, how will you win Paradise? By means of hospitality, by giving to your brothers who are poor, blind, or lame.[12]

*   *   *

Has God given us wealth? It is our duty to eat and drink so much as is sufficient, and to have enough clothes; the rest we should spend for the poor. God has not given us wealth in order that we might eat and drink to excess, and make costly clothes and build stately houses, while the poor die of starvation. Such, then, is our duty. Realize it. From today on act in this manner, and you shall be saved.[13]

*   *   *

We who are pious Christians ought to love our enemies and forgive them. We ought to offer them food and drink, and entreat God for their souls. And then we should say: "My God, I beseech Thee to forgive me, as I have forgiven my enemies."[14]

*   *   *

A man insults me, kills my father, my mother,
my brother, and then gouges out my eye. As a
Christian it is my duty to forgive him.[15]

*   *   *

If you want God to forgive you all your sins and
write your names in Paradise, say to your enemies
three times: "May God forgive you and have mercy
upon you!"[16]

Humility

The Christian needs two wings in order to soar
upward and attain Paradise: humility and love.[17]

When the first order of angels fell from angelic
glory and became demons, the other nine orders
humbled themselves and worshipped the All-Holy
Trinity, and remained in their place and rejoice
forever. We, too, my brethren, must reflect what
an evil thing pride is — that it cast down the devil
from angelic glory and he will always burn in Hell
— and that humility kept the angels in Heaven, and
they rejoice perpetually in the glory of the Holy
Trinity. Let us then, my brethren, avoid pride,
because it is the first daughter of the devil, is a path
that leads to Hell; and let us have humility, because
it is angelic, is a path that leads to Paradise.[18]

Confession

If you want to cure your soul, you need four things. The first is to forgive your enemies. The second is to confess thoroughly. The third is to blame yourself. The fourth is to resolve to sin no more.[19]

*   *   *

Glory to the all-good God for giving us a second baptism, Holy Confession, since it is impossible for an unbaptized and unconfessed man to be saved.[20]

*   *   *

If we wish to be saved, we must always blame ourselves and not attribute our wrong acts to others. And God, Who is most compassionate, will forgive us.[21]

*   *   *

If we want to benefit by Holy Communion, like the eleven good Apostles, and not to harm ourselves like the wicked Judas, we must confess sincerely and commune with fear, trembling and piety; and then we shall be illumined. But if we dare to partake of Holy Communion without Confession, defiled with sin, we put fire inside ourselves and burn.[22]

Fasting

We who are pious Christians must fast always,

but especially on Wednesday, because the Lord was
sold on that day, and on Friday, because He was
crucified on that day. Similarly, it is our duty to
fast during the Lent seasons, as the Holy Spirit
illumined the holy Fathers of the Church to decree,
in order to mortify the passions and humble the
body. Moreover, if we limit the food we eat, life
becomes easier for us.[23]

*   *   *

Fast according to your ability, pray according to
your ability, give alms according to your ability,
and always hold death before the eyes of your
mind.[24]

Virginity

Just as we humans prefer gold to silver, so the
Lord indeed likes marriage, but likes virginity more,
in order to show you that if you can preserve your
virginity and become a monk, or if you are a woman
a nun, you are fortunate and thrice blessed, you are
free from worldly things, you are like an angel.
However, if you want to preserve your virginity,
you must put as the first foundation the non-
possession-of-property *(aktemosyne)* and must
discipline your body with fasts, prayers, vigils, and
hardships in order to humble the flesh. Also, you
must flee from the world. . . . There is no other

way for the monk to be saved except by withdrawing far from the world.[25]

Woman

God created woman equal with man, not inferior.[26]

*   *   *

My Christian, you must love your wife as your companion, and not consider her as your slave, for she is a creature of God, just as you are. God was crucified for her as much as for you. You call God Father, she calls Him Father, too. Both of you have the same Faith, the same Baptism, the same Book of the Gospels, the same Holy Communion, the same Paradise to enjoy. God does not regard her as inferior to you.[27]

Keeping Sunday

Do not separate yourselves from Christ and from the Church. Do you hear the priest ringing the bells? Rise at once, wash yourselves, and go to church. Attend the Orthros attentively and likewise the Divine Liturgy.[28]

*   *   *

Six days a week we should work for these worldly

and earthly things, and on Sunday we should rest and abstain from them and work for heavenly things. That is, early in the morning we should go to church and listen to the books by the Saints and the Book of the Gospels, what Christ tells us to do. Further, we should meditate on death, Hell, and Paradise. We should think of our soul, which is more precious than the whole world, and that if we lose it we have lost everything, whereas if we gain it we have gained everything. We should wear humble clothes, eat no more than is sufficient for us, avoid idle talk, and concern ourselves with how to adorn our soul by means of good company and good morals.[29]

We should not work or do business on Sunday. The profit that you gain on Sunday is cursed .... Keep Sunday as a day dedicated to God.[30]

Jesus Prayer

This prayer should never be absent from you: "Lord Jesus Christ, Son and Logos of the living God, through the Theotokos and all the Saints, have mercy upon me, Thy sinful and unworthy servant." Always say this prayer both with your mouth and with your mind, day and night, wherever you may be, whether eating, walking, working, or sitting.

Always meditate on it, as it benefits you a great deal, frees you here[31] from every evil, delivers you there[32] from eternal Hell, and renders you worthy of going to Paradise, our heavenly country.[33]

Meditation on Death

There is no better teacher than death.[34]

*   *   *

If you want to see your fate, rise a little early in the morning and go and look at the graves of the dead. Reflect, and say to yourself: "They, too, were human beings like myself and died. Tomorrow, I also shall die. Henceforth, I will not dare to perform wicked deeds, for this will lead me to predition."[35]

*   *   *

Have death before your minds: the time when you will leave this unreal world and will go to the other one, which is eternal.[36]

Life After Death

We who are pious Christians must henceforth not weep for the dead like the impious and the unbelievers, who do not hope in the resurrection. This world, my brethren, is like a prison. When must a man rejoice? When he enters the prison or when he is being liberated from the prison? It seems to me, when he enters the prison he must weep and be sad, and when he comes out of the prison he must rejoice. Therefore, my brethren, do not grieve for the dead, but if you love them do what you can for their souls; offer liturgies, memorial services, fasts, prayers, alms.[37]

There are some who have the devil in their hearts and say that there is no resurrection, and that you have never seen a man resurrected. Now just as the Lord was able to resurrect us from the womb of our mother, so He is able to resurrect us from the womb of the earth. Do we not see the resurrection manifestly? Do we not see clearly how God resurrects the herbs of the earth every year?[38]

Teaching of the Scriptures

This, my brethren, is certain: whoever, whether man or woman, keeps the commandments of God, becomes wise and brave, and does not fear the whole world; whereas whoever does not keep them but does the will of the devil becomes a fool and a coward, and fears even his own shadow, even though he be a king and possess the whole world.[39]

*   *   *

Heed all the thoughts of the Holy Gospels, because they are all diamonds, treasures, joy, delight, eternal life.[40]

What does Christ tell us to do? To think of our sins, of death, of Hell, of Paradise, of our soul, which is more precious than the whole world, to eat and drink as much as is sufficient for us, similarly to have clothes that suffice, while the rest of our time we should spend for our soul to render it a bride of Christ. Then we should be called men, and angels on earth. If, however, we concern ourselves with eating and drinking and sinning, and adorning this gross body which tomorrow will be eaten by worms, and not with the soul, which is immortal, then we should not be called men but beasts. Therefore, make the body a servant of the soul; then you may be called men.[41]

*   *   *

The existence of many churches neither preserves nor strengthens our faith to the proper extent and in the proper manner, if those who believe in God are not enlightened by the Old and the New Testaments.[42]

*   *   *

I have found the words and the commandments of Christ pure, holy, true, splendid, brighter than the sun; and whoever believes in Christ and calls Him

God and lives in accordance with His teaching, contained in the Holy Gospels, is fortunate and thrice-blessed.[43]

*   *   *

The Holy Spirit illumined firstly the holy Prophets, and they wrote the Divine Scripture; secondly, He illumined the holy Apostles; and thirdly, He has illumined the holy Fathers, and they have explained the books of our Church, in order that we may know how to conduct ourselves.[44]

*   *   *

Our Faith has been made secure by wise and learned Saints, who both explained the Holy Scriptures precisely and have enlightened us through their divinely inspired discourses.[45]

NOTES

INTRODUCTORY

[1] Sophronios Papakyriakou, ed., *Kosma tou Aitolou Hieromartyros kai Isapostolou Didachai, Epistolai, kai Martyrion,* "Teachings, Letters, and Martyrdom of Cosmas the Aitolian, Holy Martyr and Peer of the Apostles," Athens, 1953, p. 130. Henceforth I shall refer to this book as *TLM*.

[2] Rom. 9: 3.

[3] 1 Cor. 2: 4.

[4] Augustine Kantiotis, ed., *Ho Hagios Kosmas ho Aitolos,* "Saint Cosmas Aitolos," 2nd ed., Athens, 1959, p. 62. Henceforth I shall refer to this work as *SCA*.

[5] *Ibid.,* pp. 96-97

[6] *Ibid.,* p. 66.

[7] *TLM,* p. 67.

[8] *TLM,* p. 55.

[9] *SCA,* p. 194.

[10] *SCA,* pp. 97.

[11] *SCA,* pp. 79-80

[12] *SCA,* p. 222.

[13] *TLM,* p. 34.

[14] *SCA,* p. 225.

[15] *TLM,* p. 31.

[16] *TLM,* p. 70.

[17] *SCA,* p. 8.

[18] *Kosmas Aitolos: Ho Hellen Hierapostolos,* Athens, 1961, p. 10. Cf. the following estimate of the historian Phanis Michalopoulos (1901-1960): "The modern Greek Martyrologium does not have a more wonderful, more luminous, more active, more divine figure than St. Cosmas. No matter how much we try, we do not find any fault whatsoever in his life. He was devoted completely to his mission. . . . No one contributed as much as he to the moral regeneration of his enslaved Fatherland. . . . No one worked for the Nation as much as Cosmas during the period of servitude. . . . The legend of Cosmas is still living throughout Thessaly, Macedonia, Akarnania, the Heptanese, the [Dodecanese] Islands, Albania, and South Serbia" *(Kosmas ho Aitolos, ho Ethnapostolos,* "Cosmas Aitolos, the Apostle of the Nation," Athens, 1968, pp. 191, 192, 194, 195).

[19] *Kosma Aitolou Analytike Bibliographia* (1765-1967), Athens, 1968.

[20] Augustine Kantiotis, *op. cit. ,* 3rd ed., Athens, 1966, p. 356.

THE LIFE OF ST. COSMAS

[1] Christodoulidis (d. 1856), a native of Epiros, was a faithful disciple and attendant of the Saint. He taught at the secondary schools of Ioannina, Berati, and Metsovo. His biography of Cosmas, together with an akolouthia in his honor, was first published in 1814 at Venice, under the the title, *Akolouthia kai Bios tou en Hagiois Patros hemon Kosma tou Hier-*

martyros kai Isapostolou, "Akoluthia and Life of our Father Saint Cosmas the Holy Martyr and Peer of the Apostles." The text that follows is a somewhat abridged translation I have made from the second edition, which bears the same title and appeared in 1869 at Patras.

² Cosmas received his first education at the school of Sigditsa, seventy to eighty kilometers from Mega Dendron. Then he attended the school at Vrangiana, near Agrapha.

³ Eph. 6: 4.

⁴ Cosmas taught at his native village for two years, after graduating from the school at Sigiditsa, and for a longer period at the village of Lobotina, after completing his studies at Vrangiana.

⁵ This school, which was named the Athonias Academy, was one of higher learning, a kind of college of liberal arts and school of theology. It was established in 1743 near the Monastery of Vatopedi on Mount Athos, thanks chiefly to the initiative of the Athonite monk Neophytos Kafsokalyvitis (*c.* 1702-1780), who became its first director. Neophytos subsequently taught at Chios and Bucharest, and authored many books, most of them religious. He was one of the great educators of the Greeks during the second half of the eighteenth century. The Athonias Academy reached its greatest renown under Eugene Voulgaris (1716-1806), who succeeded Neophytos Kafsokalyvitis and directed it from 1753 to 1758. Voulgaris later became Archbishop of Astrakhan and Stavropol in the Ukraine. He wrote books on diverse subjects, including logic, metaphysics, theology, mathematics, and physics. Like Kafsokalyvitis, he was one of the most influential educators of Greece.

⁶ Eugene Voulgaris.

⁷ The term *ascesis* occurs frequently in the writings of the Greek Church Fathers, and Eastern Orthodoxy has rightly been characterized as an *ascetic* religion. However, the term ascesis has acquired a distorted meaning in modern popular

usage, "implying an element of self-maceration." Actually, this Greek word means *exercise,* either physical or mental, spiritual, and its aim within the Orthodox Church is to perfect the soul and to render the body a sound and obedient servant of the soul. Its ultimate end is *theosis,* "deification," union with God. There is nothing morbid in ascesis thus conceived and practiced under the guidance of an experienced and wise teacher. Ascesis becomes negative when it is used without discretion and is viewed as an end in itself, and not as a means. Ascesis is of two major kinds, bodily and spiritual. Bodily ascesis consists of such practices as fasting, prostrations, vigils, and psalmodizing, while spiritual ascesis consists of such "work" as inner attention, guarding of the mind, heart and senses, and prayer of the mind and heart.

[8] He left the school after having studied there for five years, according to some sources, for eight years according to others.

[9] On Mount Athos.

[10] At tonsure his name was changed from Constas to Cosmas, in accordance with the custom in Eastern Orhodox monasticism of giving another name to one who embraces the monastic life, thus symbolizing that the old self has died and a new one has been born, and helping the monk (or nun) stop associating himself with the old personality, psychologically so closely connected with the name.

[11] 1 Cor. 10: 24.

[12] In 1760.

[12] In 1760.

[13] Chrysanthos, an Archimandrite, taught for a time at the Patriarchal School at Constantinople, and later became director of the school in Naxos, one of the Cyclades Islands. As a teacher in Naxos, he played an important role in the education and character formation of another Saint, Nicodemos the Hagiorite.

[14] Typically, a skete on Athos is a settlement of hermits in

the neighborhood of a common church, by which is the dwelling of the Prior *(Dikaios)* of the settlement and a guesthouse.

[15] Lefkas, one of the Ionian Islands.

[16] Christ's disciples.

[17] Zante.

[18] In Corfu, as well as in Zakynthos, the wealthy, who allied themselves with the Venetian overloards and exploited the common people, reducing them to a state of misery, were strongly censured by Cosmas for their greed and lack of Christian love. The effect of this was, on the one hand, to excite the indignation of the people against them, and on the other, to arouse the fear of the Venetians and the wealthy about the status quo.

[19] Orthodox Baptism calls for full immersion, and hence large baptismal basins are required, if it is to be performed properly.

[20] In accordance with Paul's statement: "Every woman that prays or prophesies with her head uncovered dishonors her head" (1 Cor. 11: 5).

[21] In one of his sermons, Cosmas says: "It is natural for a man when he reaches the age of fifty to leave his beard. Yet I see here old men of sixty and eighty still shaving. Aren't you ashamed to shave? Did not God, Who gave the beard, know? . . . If you see a man of thirty who has grown a beard, and one who is fifty or sixty or a hundred and shaves, give to the man with the beard a place of greater honor than to the one who shaves, both in church and at the table" *(SCA,* pp. 85-86).

[22] The Saint recommended the use of the prayer-rope during the practice of the Prayer of Jesus: "Now I enjoin you to do this: all of you take a prayer-rope, which should have one hundred and three knots, and at each knot say: 'Lord Jesus Christ, Son and Logos of the living God, through the Theotokos and all the Saints have mercy upon me, Thy sinful

and unworthy servant' " (*SCA,* p. 226).

²³ A locality in Albania northeast of Aghioi Saranta.

²⁴ A Turkish word meaning "herd," used by the Ottoman Turks to denote their Christian subjects.

²⁵ Psalm 65 (66): 12.

²⁶ In 1809.

²⁷ Velegrada was the ecclesiastical name of Berati.

ON GOD

¹ Augustine N. Kantiotis, *Ho Hagios Kosmas ho Aitolos* (3rd, augmented edition, Athens 1966), *Didache* 1, p. 92; cf. *Didache* 6, p. 209. All citations of Cosmas' *Didachai* are from Kantiotis' book. The first number refers to the number of the didache. It is followed by the page reference.

² Kantiotis, 1, 92; cf. 1, 93; 5, 191.

³ *Ibid.,* 1, 92-93; cf. 2, 142; 6, 209-210; 8, 265.

⁴ *Ibid.,* 1, 95; 5, 191.

⁵ *Ibid.,* 1, 93. Cf. St. John Damascene: "For the invisible things of God, since the creation of the world, are seen and apprehended in created things. We see images in creation which faintly reveal to us the reflections of God, as when, for instance, we speak of the Holy and eternal Trinity being imaged by the sun, light, and ray" (Migne, *PatrologiaGraeca,* 94, col. 1241B-C).

⁶ *Ibid.,* 8, 298.

⁷ *Ibid.,* 1, 93.

⁸ *Ibid.,* 1, 93; 5, 191.

⁹ *Ibid.,* 1, 92-93; cf.5, 204; 7, 232.

¹⁰ *Ibid.,* 1, 95; 4, 172; 7, 234.

[11] *Ibid.,* 1, 85; 3, 134; 6, 207.

[12] *Ibid.,* 1, 92, 95, 102, 103, 106, 110, 112; 2, 137, 141; 4, 157, 158; 5, 192, 194, 196, 201, 203, etc.

[13] *Ibid.,* 1, 95; cf, 6, 210.

[14] *Ibid.,* 7, 234.

[15] *Ibid.,* 1,100, 101, 114; 3, 137; 4, 182; 5, 193.

[16] *Ibid.,* 1, 93, 95.

[17] *Ibid.,* 1, 93, 95, 100.

[18] *Ibid.,* 1, 114; 5, 193.

[19] *Ibid.,* 1, 114; cf. 2, 136; 5, 193.

[20] *Ibid.,* 1, 95; cf. 1, 96, 100; 6, 209.

[21] *Ibid.,* 1, 92, 117, etc.

[22] *Ibid.,* 4, 177.

[23] *Ibid.,* 8, 288.

[24] *Ibid.,* 2, 121.

[25] *Ibid.,* 1, 89; 2, 121; 4, 172; 8, 298.

[26] *Ibid.,* 2, 121.

[27] *Ibid.,* 1, 93.

[28] *Ibid.,* 1, 85; 3, 134; 6, 207.

[29] *Ibid.,* 1, 89; 3, 134; 6, 207.

[30] *Ibid.,* 2, 121.

[31] *Ibid.,* 1, 89.

[32] *Ibid.,* 1, 85, 108, 118; 2, 134; 4, 156, 179; 6, 207; 7, 220, 223, 239, 256; 8, 259.

[33] *Ibid.,* 11: 29.

[34] *Symbouleutikon Encheiridion* (2nd ed., Athens, 1885), p. 145. Cf. St. Nectarios Kephalas, *To Gnothi Sauton,* "Self-Knowledge" (2nd ed., Athens, 1962), p. 183.

[35] Kantiotis. 1, 85.

[36] *Ibid.,* 1, 85; cf. 1, 114; 5, 206.

[37] *Ibid.,* 1, 93.

[38] *Ibid.,* 1, 92; cf. 4, 170.

[39] *Ibid.,* 2, 135; cf. 7, 221.

[40] *Ibid.,* 5, 189

[41] *Ibid.,* 1, 86; cf. 6, 208; 8, 263.

[42] *Ibid.,* 4, 164

[43] *Ibid.,* 3, 150-151.

[44] *Ibid.,* 6, 213-214.

[45] *Ibid.,* 8, 273.

[46] John 14: 6-7

[47] *Ibid.,* 3, 14-141; 6, 213; 8, 273.

[48] *Ibid.,* 8, 273.

[49] *Ibid.*

[50] *Ibid.,* 1, 95-96.

[51] *Ibid.,* 1, 95.

[52] *Ibid.,* 1, 96.

[53] *Ibid.,* 1, 93-94.

[54] *Ibid.,* 1, 102.

[55] *Ibid.,* 3, 150-151.

[56] *Ibid.,* 1, 117; 4, 180; 6, 213.

⁵⁷ *Ibid.,* 1, 110-111; 6, 213.

⁵⁸ *Ibid.,* 1, 93, 119; 2, 141-142.

HEAVEN AND HELL

¹ Kantiotis, *op. cit.,* p. 85.

² *Ibid.,* p. 119.

³ *Ibid.,* p. 106. Cf. p. 94.

⁴ *Ibid.,* p. 133.

⁵ *Ibid.,* p. 180. Cf. p. 213.

⁶ *Ibid.,* pp. 262-263.

⁷ *Ibid.,* pp. 102-103.

⁸ *Ibid.,* p. 97.

⁹ *Ibid.,* pp. 97-98. Cf. p. 137.

¹⁰ *Ibid.,* p. 100.

¹¹ *Ibid.,* pp. 160-161.

¹² *Ibid.,* pp. 161-162.

¹³ *Ibid.,* p. 278.

¹⁴ *Ibid.,* pp. 123-124.

¹⁵ *Ibid.,* pp. 162-163.

¹⁶ *Ibid.,* p. 94.

¹⁷ *Ibid.,* pp. 95-96.

¹⁸ *Ibid.,* pp. 218-219.

¹⁹ *Ibid.,* pp. 167-168.

²⁰ *Ibid.,* p. 251.

21 *Ibid.,* p. 163.

22 *Ibid.,* p. 137.

23 *Ibid.,* pp. 169-170.

24 *Ibid.,* p. 278.

25 *Ibid.,* pp. 140-141.

26 *Ibid.,* p. 213.

27 *Ibid.,* p. 273

28 *Ibid.,* pp. 281-282.

29 *Ibid.,* pp. 93-94

30 *Ibid.,* p. 93.

31 *Ibid.,* pp. 93-94.

32 *Ibid.,* p. 181.

PROPHECIES

1 *Ho Hagios Kosmas ho Aitolos* ("Saint Cosmas Aitolos"), 5th, augmented edition, Athens, 1976, pp. 99-107.

2 Kantiotis, *Ho Hagios Kosmas ho Aitolos* ("Saint Cosmas Aitolos"), 6th, improved edition, Athens, 1981, pp. 336-352; Giolias, *Ho Kosmas Aitolos kai he Epoche tou* ("Cosmas Aitolos and his Time"), Athens 1972, pp. 429-435.

3 Kantiotis, *op. cit.,* p. 318.

4 *Ibid.,*

5 *Ibid.,* p. 325.

6 *Ibid.,* p. 328.

7 L. K. Kataphygiotis, *Ethnomartyres Klerikoi kai ho Pater Kosmas,* Karditsa, 1940, p. 124.

8 In his above mentioned book, p. 332.

SELECTED PASSAGES

[1] *TLM,* p. 32.

[2] *Ibid.*

[3] *TLM,* p. 33.

[4] *SCA,* p. 69.

[5] *SCA,* p. 71.

[6] Matt. 22: 40.

[7] *TLM,* p. 35.

[8] *TLM,* p. 36.

[9] *SCA,* p. 73.

[10] *TLM,* pp. 109-110.

[11] *TLM,* p. 49.

[12] *TLM,* p. 101.

[13] *TLM,* p. 121.

[14] *TLM,* p. 82.

[15] *SCA,* p. 186.

[16] *SCA,* p. 156.

[17] *SCA,* pp. 79-80.

[18] *SCA,* p. 79.

[19] *TLM,* pp. 85-86

[20] *SCA,* p. 269.

[21] *SCA,* p. 91.

[22] *TLM,* p. 83.

[23] *SCA,* p. 167.

²⁴ *TLM,* pp. 135-136.

²⁵ *TLM,* p. 129.

²⁶ *SCA,* p. 84.

²⁷ *TLM,* p. 44-45.

²⁸ *TLM,* p. 149.

²⁹ *TLM,* pp. 41-42.

³⁰ *TLM,* p. 90.

³¹ On earth.

³² In the after-life.

³³ *TLM,* p. 52.

³⁴ *SCA,* p. 84.

³⁵ *SCA,* p. 243.

³⁶ *SCA,* p.99.

³⁷ *TLM,* p. 88. The Orthodox Church teaches that through such acts on behalf of the departed the sufferings of the souls that have descended to Hell are alleviated, and those who have not committed mortal sins may be saved.

³⁸ *TLM,* p. 89.

³⁹ *TLM,* p. 46.

⁴⁰ *TLM,* p. 80.

⁴¹ *SCA,* p. 82.

⁴² *TLM,* p. 137.

⁴³ *TLM,* p. 142.

⁴⁴ *TLM,* p. 67.

⁴⁵ Phanis Michalopoulos, *op. cit.,* pp. 120-121.

SELECTED BIBLIOGRAPHY

Christodoulidis, Sapphiros, *Akolouthia kai Bios tou en Hagiois Patros hemon Kosma tou Hieromartyros kai Isapostolou* ("Akolouthia and Life of our Father among Saints Cosmas the Hieromartyr and Peer of the Apostles"). Venice, 1814. 2nd edition, Patras, 1869.

Evangelidis, Tryphon, *Kosmas ho Aitolos ho Isapostolos, Bios kai Erga* ("Cosmas Aitolos the Peer of the Apostles, his Life and Works"). Athens, 1897.

Giolias, Markos A., *Ho Kosmas Aitolos kai he Epoche tou* ("Cosmas Aitolos and his Epoch"). Athens, 1972.

Kantiotis, Augustine, *Ho Hagios Kosmas ho Aitolos: Synaxarion — Didachai — Propheteiai — Akolouthia* ("Saint Cosmas Aitolos: His Life, *Didachai,* Prophecies, and Akolouthia"). 2nd edition, Athens, 1959;

3rd, augmented edition, 1966. 6th, improved edition, 1981. (1st edition Volos, 1950.)

Kataphygiotis, Lampros K., *Ethnomartyres Klerikoi kai ho Pater Kosmas* ("National-Martyr Clerics and Father Cosmas"). Karditsa, 1940.

Kontoglou, Photios, *Pege Zoes* ("Fount of Life"). Athens, 1951, pp. 101-110.

Michalopoulos, Phanis, *Kosmas ho Aitolos, ho Ethnapostolos* ("Cosmas Aitolos, the Apostle of the Nation"). Athens, 1968.

Micragiannanitis, Gerasimos, *Akolouthia kai Bios tou hagiou Hieromartyros kai Isapostolou Kosma tou Aitolou* ("Akolouthia and Life of the holy Hieromartyr and Peer of the Apostles Cosmas the Aitolian"). Athens, 1966. Revised and augmented edition 1971.

Papakyriakou, Sophronios, *Kosma tou Aitolou Hieromartyros kai Isapostolou Didachai, Epistolai, kai Martyrion* ("The *Didachai,* Letters, and Martyrdom of Cosmas the Hieromartyr and Peer of the Apostles"). Athens, 1953.

Salamankas, Dem. S., *Ho Gnostos Kalogeros Kosmas* ("The Well-known Monk Cosmas"). Athens, 1952.

Sardelis, Kostas, *Kosma Aitolou Analytike Bibliographia 1765-1967* ("Analytical Bibliography of Cosmas

Aitolos — 1765-1967"). Athens, 1968. 2nd, augmented edition, covering the period 1765-1973, Athens, 1974.

Vaporis, N. M., *Father Kosmas: The Apostle of the Poor.* Brookline, Massachusetts, 1977.

Vasilopoulos, Haralambos, *Ho Hagios Kosmas ho Aitolos* ("Saint Cosmas Aitolos"). 5th, augmented edition, Athens, 1976. (1st edition Athens, 1961.)

INDEX

THE OTHER SEVEN VOLUMES OF THE SERIES *MODERN ORTHODOX SAINTS* PUBLISHED BY THE INSTITUTE FOR BYZANTINE AND MODERN GREEK STUDIES

Vol. 2, ST. MACARIOS OF CORINTH

An account of the life, character and message of St. Macarios of Corinth (1731-1805) — Archbishop of Corinth, guardian of sacred Tradition, reviver of Orthodox mysticism *(hesychasm)*, compiler of the *Philokalia,* spiritual striver, enlightener and guide, and trainer of martyrs — together with selections from three of his publications, compiled, translated and edited with an Introduction and Notes by C. Cavarnos, 2nd ed., 1977. 118 pp., 1 plate.
ISBN 0-914744-35-6 (Paperbound).

Vol. 3, ST. NICODEMOS THE HAGIORITE

An account of the life, character and teaching of St. Nicodemos the Hagiorite (1749-1809) — great theologian and teacher of the Orthodox Church, enlightener, reviver of hesychasm, moralist, canonist, hagiologist, and writer of liturgical poetry — together with a comprehensive list of his publications and selections from them, translated and edited with an Introduction and Notes by C. Cavarnos, 2nd edition, 1979, 167 pp., 1 plate.
ISBN 0-914744-41-0 (Cloth).   ISBN 0-914744-68-2 (Paperbound).

Vol. 4, ST. NIKEPHOROS OF CHIOS

An account of the life, character and message of St. Nikephoros of Chios (1750-1821) — outstanding writer of liturgical poetry and lives of saints, educator, spiritual striver, and trainer of martyrs — together with a comprehensive list of his publications, selections from them, and brief biographies of eleven neomartyrs and other Orthodox saints who are treated in his works. By C. Cavarnos. 1976. 124 pp. 1 plate.
ISBN 0-914744-32-1 (Cloth), 0-914744-33-X (Paperbound).

Vol. 5, ST. SERAPHIM OF SAROV

An account of the life, character and message of St. Seraphim of Sarov (1759-1833) — widely beloved mystic, healer, comforter, and spiritual guide — together with a very edifying Conversation with his disciple Nicholas Motovilov on the acquisition of the grace of the Holy Spirit, and the Saint's Spiritual Counsels. By C. Cavarnos and Mary-Barbara Zeldin. 1980. 167 pp. 1 plate.
ISBN 0-9144-47-X (Cloth), 0-914744-48-8 (Paperbound).

Vol. 6, ST. ARSENIOS OF PAROS

An account of the life, character, message and miracles of St. Arsenios of Paros (1800-1877) — remarkable confessor, spiritual guide, educator, ascetic, miracle-worker, and healer — together with some of his counsels. Compiled, translated and edited with an Introduction, Notes, and Bibliography by C. Cavarnos. 1978. 123 pp. 1 plate.
ISBN 0-914744-39 (Cloth), 0-914744-40-2 (Paperbound).

Vol. 7, ST. NECTARIOS OF AEGINA

An account of the life, character, and teaching of St. Nectarios of Aegina (1846-1920) — educator, theologian, spiritual guide, miracle-worker and healer — together with a comprehensive list of his writings, selections from them translated and edited with an extensive and illuminating Introduction and Notes by C. Cavarnos, and in addition a chapter on the miracles of the Saint and an essay on his teaching on God. 1981. 222 pp. 1 plate.
ISBN 0-914744-53-4 (Cloth), 0-914744-54-2 (Paperbound).

Vol. 8, ST. SAVVAS THE NEW, OF KALYMNOS

Remarkable Ascetic, Confessor, Spiritual Guide, Iconographer, Miracle-Worker and Healer (1862-1947). An account of his Life, Character, Message and Miracles, together with his nine Definitions of true Monastic Conduct and photographs of many of his holy icons. By C. Cavarnos. 1985. 144 pp. 23 illus.
ISBN 0-914744-62-3 (Cloth), 0-914744-63-1 (Paperbound).